Social Media Shaping e-Publishing and Academia

Nashrawan Taha · Rizik Al-Sayyed
Ja'far Alqatawna · Ali Rodan
Editors

Social Media Shaping e-Publishing and Academia

Springer

Editors
Nashrawan Taha
Department of Library and Information Science, Educational Science Faculty
The University of Jordan
Amman
Jordan

Rizik Al-Sayyed
Department of Business Information Technology, King Abdullah II School of Information Technology (KASIT)
The University of Jordan
Amman
Jordan

Ja'far Alqatawna
Department of Business Information Technology, King Abdullah II School of Information Technology (KASIT)
The University of Jordan
Amman
Jordan

Ali Rodan
Department of Business Information Technology, King Abdullah II School of Information Technology (KASIT)
The University of Jordan
Amman
Jordan

ISBN 978-3-319-55353-5 ISBN 978-3-319-55354-2 (eBook)
DOI 10.1007/978-3-319-55354-2

Library of Congress Control Number: 2017934872

Printed on acid-free paper

This Springer imprint is published by Springer Nature
The registered company is Springer International Publishing AG
The registered company address is: Gewerbestrasse 11, 6330 Cham, Switzerland

Preface

The popularity of various types of Online Social Networks (OSNs) is increasing dramatically. Nowadays, platforms such as Facebook, Twitter, LinkedIn, and YouTube are used in business, education, and social activities by billions of users around the world. In fact, several factors contributed to this ever-increasing popularity. Obviously, many of these platforms mimic real social relationships and give their users the opportunities to communicate over a very convenient online medium, meeting new friends, and sharing a large amount of information. Moreover, OSNs empowered online users with the capability for instant publishing of their own generated multimedia content. In the era of Online Social Media (OSM), publishing for the 'inter' world has become one click away. With less restriction, filtering or censorship, publishing has become very tempting for millions of users. In the context of libraries, social media has an impact on shaping library services and resources. E-publishing is one of the library aspects that can be affected by social media, where the library e-content can be augmented and better shared via social media.

The main aim of this book is to present the current state of the art in the field of e-publishing and social media. The book discusses a relatively new research topic that will be useful to researchers in the area of social media and e-publishing.

The book mainly discusses the role of social media in shaping e-publishing. It includes four main parts; namely, Social Media in Libraries and Information Centers, Social Media and e-publishing Usages in e-learning, Information Retrieval in Social Media, and Information Security in Social Media.

The first part discusses *Social Media in Libraries and Information Centers*, where three case studies are presented. The first chapter of this part reports the experience and recommendations of two librarians in a large U.S. university library for using social media as a library communication tool, especially Facebook and Twitter. The researchers then make recommendations for branch library and subject librarian social media usage. The second chapter discusses a second case study about the impact of social networks on information consumption and usage. The researchers have studied a bibliographic database (e-Marefa) to examine how social media can improve the value of an academic article. The research showed that an article can be 'virally' downloaded and read when shared via social media. The third chapter explains the role that social media had on Wikipedia where analysis of how the presumption of information in social media shaped Wikipedia is explored.

The second part presents new researches in the field of *Social Media and e-Publishing Usages in e-Learning*. The major ideas presented in these research study chapters include how Social Network Sites (SNS) increase the activity and efficiency of e-learning by assessing the risks and advantages of using these networks, how SNS use IPython to support educators in teaching the fundamentals of web scraping, how SNS are used to support the learning and academic activities in universities and how SNS shaped the e-content for the present generation, and how SNS as used more as means of socialization than as a learning medium so that sharing and exchanging information and e-publishing have become the norm; examples include blogs, e-books, e-journals, online newspapers, while digital library usage was relegated to a minor position.

The third part discusses *Information Retrieval in Social Media*. Three chapters are presented to discuss the investigating and designing of new Information Retrieval (IR) models in the context of social media. The first chapter develops a defeasible description logic system that can represent a flexible publication ontology which can support intelligent queries. In the second chapter, authors discuss a retrieval method that can meet users' requests and handle their diversity by investigating several techniques to support users in searching and navigating the full texts of digitized books and complementary social media in order to enhance the user book search experience. They employed the INEX SBS track which uses professional metadata and user generated metadata (social media content) to enhance the retrieval process for books.

The fourth part of the book covers *Security and Privacy in the Era of Social Media*. It has one chapter which discusses some of the current research in the field of online social networks security. It presents different attacks that are especially relevant to online social networks. Moreover, it highlights some methods and precautions available to tackle these attacks. A discussion of the trade-off between services and security is also given in the light of stakeholders' rights and responsibilities. Accordingly, authors of the chapters argue that there is a need for suggesting models and technical solutions in the light of the emerging threats highlighted in the chapter. Possible future research directions related to privacy, Sybil attacks, social engineering, spam, malware, and botnet attacks are discussed.

We would like to finally convey our gratitude to the authors of the accepted chapters and the reviewers of these chapters. We are grateful to the University of Jordan Library for their help and support. We are also grateful to Springer for their support in publishing this book.

Amman, Jordan
December 2016

Nashrawan Taha
Rizik Al-Sayyed
Ja'far Alqatawna
Ali Rodan

Contents

Part I
Social Media in Libraries and Information Centers

Social media use has become an integral part of everyone's daily life. The number of digital resources in these platforms is exponentially increasing, where user are generating, modifying, and sharing this content. The greater reliance on social media has changed the role of libraries and information centers as traditional repositories of information. Social media can effectively be integrated into library services to outreach the learning community. In fact, many libraries and information centers have already embraced social media tools to enhance their services and engage their users. Social media can be beneficial in promoting library services and in connecting libraries with their users regardless of location.

Social media use is changing the role of libraries and information professionals. Librarians have now a crucial role in directing the learning community through the complex digital information environment. With the 'born digital' content, created and shared via social media, e-publishing became an important topic that needs to be researched and explored. Social media can help libraries share their e-content, such as e-books, e-theses, and e-periodicals with a wider community.

This part presents three case study chapters of using social media in libraries and information centers. The first chapter discusses a case study of a large U.S. university library, where the experiences and recommendations of two librarians for using social media as a library communication tool were explored. The researchers have used personal observation in Facebook and Twitter to make recommendations for branch library and subject librarian social media usage.

The second chapter outlines another case study about the impact of social networks on information consumption and usage. The researchers have studied a bibliographic database (e-Marefa) to examine how social media can improve the value of an academic article 'virally', where their research showed a significant increase of the number of times that an article can be downloaded and read when shared via social media.

The third chapter has studied the role that social media had on Wikipedia where the authors have conducted an analysis of how the presumption of information in social media shaped Wikipedia.

Nashrawan Taha

Reaching Your Community via Social Media: Academic Libraries and Librarians Using Facebook and Twitter for Outreach

Deborah J. Margolis and Emily A. Treptow

Abstract In the case studies presented in this chapter, two librarians from a large U.S. university library share experiences and recommendations for using social media as a library communication tool. Emily Treptow managed Facebook and Twitter accounts for a branch business library. Deborah Margolis uses a personal Facebook account as a liaison librarian, and reports on colleagues' Twitter usage. In this chapter, Margolis and Treptow primarily use personal observation to make recommendations for branch library and subject librarian social media usage. Choosing a social media platform, best practices for using social media (such as how much, when, and what to post), and assessing your social media use will be discussed. Considerations including audience, privacy, content and format of posts, frequency and timing of posts, and time commitment of the librarian will be addressed.

1 Introduction

Social media can help university libraries and librarians connect with their communities. It can be used to promote library collections and services and keep the library in the mind of the library user. Social media provides an avenue to communicate with users in addition to the more traditional media such as websites, newsletters, and advertisements in campus newspapers. Perhaps axiomatic, it is

---

"E.A. Treptow formerly at Michigan State University currently at University of Chicago."

D.J. Margolis (✉)
Margolis Middle East Studies & Anthropology Librarian,
Michigan State University, East Lansing, USA
e-mail: deborahm@msu.edu

E.A. Treptow
Treptow Business & Economics Librarian for Instruction & Outreach,
University of Chicago, Chicago, USA
e-mail: etreptow@uchicago.edu

N. Taha et al. (eds.), *Social Media Shaping e-Publishing and Academia*,
DOI 10.1007/978-3-319-55354-2_1

important to note that social media differs from traditional library media in that it can lead to exchange and spread of ideas, rather than just a one-way producer to consumer model. Here we will provide case studies describing the implementation and use of Facebook and Twitter by a branch/subject library and liaison/subject librarians at Michigan State University, sharing best practices for using social media as a library communication tool.

Michigan State University is a large public research university with 50,000 students and 17 degree-granting colleges, located in the Midwestern United States. It was founded in 1855 with the mission to share agricultural research with the state of Michigan; today, Michigan State University (MSU) is active in research and teaching both locally and globally.

The MSU Libraries are organized into a Main Library and branches, as well as into divisions such as public services, technical services, and collections. The work of building and maintaining library collections is divided among subject, or, liaison librarians. Liaison librarians in recent years have communicated with their faculty and students by email and email lists, attending and presenting at academic department faculty meetings and lectures, providing orientation and library instruction/information literacy sessions, meeting with individual faculty members and students, and organizing events and exhibits in collaboration with teaching/research faculty. Social media offers an additional way to connect with faculty and students in our subject areas. At the time of this writing, the MSU Libraries are moving toward centralization of their main Facebook and Twitter accounts using Hootsuite, which allows prewriting and scheduling of posts. At the same time, liaison librarians, library units, and branch libraries have their own social media accounts which they manage independently.

The Gast Business Library is one of the five branch libraries at Michigan State University and primarily serves MSU's Broad College of Business and The School of Hospitality, with roughly 6,000 undergraduate students, 800 graduate students, and 125 faculty members [1]. Over 20% of Broad and Hospitality students are international students, most of them are Chinese. In August 2012, the Gast Business Library launched a Facebook and Twitter account after researching and writing a social media proposal, which included recommended platforms, target audience, sources for content, and an initial schedule. The branch librarian referenced the key online magazine *Social Media Examiner* when writing the branch social media proposal.

2 Choosing a Social Media Platform

2.1 Audience

Before choosing a social media platform, it is worthwhile to consider your audience. Do you have a primary clientele which you wish to reach? Do you wish to reach faculty, graduate students, undergraduate students, librarians and library workers, or a wider community? Thinking about your audience can affect the social media platform you choose, as well as the content you post. Unlike accounts that represent university libraries, branch and liaison librarians have the ability to target their content to a more specific audience. The business branch librarian was able to focus on content that would be of interest to business students and faculty. However, this more targeted audience was still broad in terms of their preferred social media platform and their social media habits. This made Facebook and Twitter the ideal platforms to start with because these social media platforms reach the most users. As of March 31, 2015, there were 1.44 billion active monthly users on Facebook [2]. As of the same date, Twitter had 302 million active monthly users [3]. It is worth noting that because of its large international student population, the business librarian opted to also use WeChat as a way to reach Chinese students, a prominent subset of the target population who are not active on Facebook or Twitter.

2.2 *Privacy*

Using a personal Facebook or Twitter account as a liaison librarian necessitates some additional privacy considerations. Do you want your posts to be available to anyone, or do you want to approve who sees your original or forwarded content? If students are part of your intended audience, understand that they may not want librarians participating in their private social lives. The Middle East Studies librarian began her Facebook account as a way to reach out to the undergraduate and graduate students in the Arabic class she was taking. She observed that only some students in the class chose to be 'friends' with the subject librarian on Facebook. Fellow librarians and faculty may also prefer to connect with actual friends and family on Facebook, and may maintain separate social media accounts, one for professional interests and one for personal matters.

Creating a page for your library as an organization on Facebook allows a separation between the institutional and the personal in social media. Whether you decide to use a personal account or create an institutional presence for your library, unit, or function, it is recommended to share some of your personality. Strive to let your community hear your unique voice.

2.3 *Time Commitment*

Maintaining a well-curated social media account takes time. Before creating any account, consider the time it will take. It is better to have one account that promotes engagement than multiple accounts that end up being neglected. Reading and responding to your community's posts is part of participating effectively in social media and also requires a daily time commitment. Not responding in a timely fashion could discourage the user from engaging with your account again.

3 Social Media Best Practices

3.1 Content of Posts

Library or librarian postings may include notices of new books, databases, or exhibits; library events and workshops; or changes to library hours or access. Librarians can help get the word out about academic departmental activities taking place outside the library, as well as about community activities related to his or her subject or area. The Middle East Studies liaison's Facebook page attempts to function as a virtual space where students, faculty, and community members can learn about Middle East Studies lectures or other events of interest. The Business Library's posts range from event information, service updates, and research tips to interesting shared content from relevant business and news publications.

Library-centered content is important and should be posted, but it is also a good idea to share and repost external content that your community cares about. A survey of 28 academic libraries' social media accounts showed that while library-related posts made up 70% of all posts, it only motivated engagement (likes, comments, shares/retweets) 40% of the time. Shared content (for example sharing a Facebook post or retweeting a tweet) made up 11% of the content but garnered responses 70% of the time [4]. The Business Library has observed this type of success when sharing posts from the MSU community, including MSU's institutional accounts, the Broad College of Business, and MSU sports. In their 2015 paper 'Libraries Using Twitter Better: Insights on Engagement from Food Trucks,' Katie Emery and Todd Schifeling recommend that libraries should be more active in sharing and retweeting, mentioning other users (using Twitter hashtags), and using more images in their posts [5].

For library accounts, social media is also a wonderful way to build a community among library staff and student workers. The business librarian observed that some of the Gast Business Library's most popular posts have included photos of student workers. Even after they have graduated, former Business Library student workers are staying connected to the library through social media. Be sure to get permission from students and staff before you post their photos. In order to remain in accordance with the U.S. federal law FERPA (Family Educational Rights and Privacy Act), the branch librarian had all students sign a document stating they were giving permission for their photo to be used.

Emery and Schifeling found that there was not significant engagement among institutional library Twitter accounts; academic libraries have not connected with other peer institutions using Twitter [5] (p. 453). However, the liaison librarian feels she has been able to maintain and build relationships with fellow Middle East

Studies librarians and libraries via Facebook, after meeting in person at the Middle East Librarians Association annual conference. Twitter is often used during conferences to connect with those at the conference as well as those not able to attend. In addition, social media can be used to connect with local public and academic librarians, which has led to new collaborative efforts, such as an exhibition from the MSU Libraries traveling for exhibit at the local public libraries. Despite this librarian's experience networking on Facebook, she has noticed that most librarians at our university use Facebook personally rather than professionally, and Twitter is more likely to be used for work.

Digital scholarship librarian Thomas Padilla shares his latest blog posts via his Twitter account. Other librarians may be more comfortable following the Twitter accounts and/or Facebook pages of faculty and researchers without actively participating in the conversation taking place. If you are reticent to post original content, you can share or retweet others' posts, which, as we have noted, can be an effective way of generating interest. MSU's Education Librarian, Jill Morningstar, uses Twitter to learn what is happening within MSU's College of Education by following faculty and graduate students. Twitter and Facebook can function for librarians as a current awareness tool for learning about topics in your subject field.

One way that librarians can make a valuable contribution to a social media conversation is by providing information to students and faculty relevant to their research interests. The branch librarian and subject librarians have been asked reference questions on social media, and have taken the initiative to provide information when an information need has been voiced. The librarian may draw attention to a resource in the library collection, or offer an authoritative and/or unusual source of news or data which their audience may not be familiar with. Libraries are currently using URLs in their posts on Twitter, which fits naturally into our roles as information providers [5].

It is advised to check your institution's and library's policies on professional use of social media before beginning or expanding your professional presence on social media. Michigan State University's guidelines for social media emphasize that opinions shared on social media will be considered by readers as representing the university [6]. While some librarians may wish to remain neutral on political issues so as not to alienate members of their communities with varied viewpoints, it is difficult and perhaps not even desirable to refrain from commenting on the most important social and political topics of the day, such as civil and human rights. If such topics fall within the purview of libraries, information, and/or our subject areas, the subject librarian feels we have a responsibility to engage, and risk irrelevancy by not doing so. This may be more or less feasible based on a particular librarian's national or institutional context. If you manage an institutional account, you are officially representing your university. The branch librarian opted to avoid potentially controversial topics, such as those relating to religion and politics, when posting for the Gast Business Library.

3.2 *Format, Length, and Frequency of Posts*

In addition to content, it is also important to consider format. While Twitter limits you to 140 characters, Facebook posts can get lengthy, with an allowance for over 63,000 characters [7]. Recent studies have noted what character length promotes the most engagement on Facebook and Twitter. Studies from two different social media analytics firms found that retweets spiked when tweets were between 71 and 100 characters and Jeff Bullas found that Facebook posts that were 80 characters or less received 66% higher engagement [8]. Posts with images also create higher reach and engagement. 87% of shared Facebook posts were photos. No other post type accounted for more than 45% of shared posts [9].

Consistency helps when it comes to thinking about when and how often to post. On Facebook, two posts of well-curated content a week is a good starting point. The branch librarian observed engagement of the Business Library's posts and found that followers were most engaged on Thursday afternoons. The liaison librarian using Facebook observed that while she had more free time on Friday (the last day of the working week in the U.S.), posting on Fridays did not garner much response. The digital scholarship librarian who is active on Twitter will tweet at any time, any day of the week, as Twitter is a primary mode of engagement for that librarian's field of digital humanities.

For the more traditional function of advertising events, we recommend posting major events one month ahead of the event, and then once a week in the period leading up to the event. Sharing articles or websites related to the event may increase interest, and as previously recommended, include an image for increased engagement. In a large, decentralized university such as ours, appreciation for sharing events happening in different units on campus has been voiced by the librarians' social media community. When promoting an event that may be of interest to specific units on campus, the branch librarian noticed it was beneficial to reach out to other social media coordinators to ask if they will help promote the event, and also to tag them in posts.

4 Assessing Your Social Media Use

In order to track growth, the branch librarian has noted monthly reach and engagement statistics since creating the Gast Business Library's Facebook and Twitter accounts. She observed that both accounts have shown slow but steady growth since their creation. The business librarian also observed that the Facebook account's engagement and reach continues to grow as more posts involving students and staff are incorporated into the content. From looking at the statistics, she concluded that tagging people in posts has also helped to increase reach. The branch librarian has found that Twitter engagement is at its highest when the Business Library tweets more and especially when there is interaction with other accounts. The branch librarian also found it useful to look at analytics of successful individual posts and tweets. Facebook only provides analytics for posts on page accounts. To see analytics for personal Facebook accounts, Google Analytics is available. Twitter also provides analytics for tweets. Seeing what type of posts created the highest reach and engagement informed changes in the branch's social media strategy.

5 Conclusion

Social media is truly invaluable due to its potential for new and enhanced relationships with your library's community. For the branch librarian, the implementation and the curation of the Gast Business Library's social media accounts has led to further insights on best practices. She has used these social media accounts as a start of a renewed focus on the marketing of the library's services and resources. Both the branch and liaison librarian have had positive experiences reaching their users with social media, and will continue to explore strategies that can be leveraged in the future to increase connections and inspire conversations with their communities.

References

1. Broad College of Business (2014) Fast facts. Retrieved from https://broad.msu.edu/information/fastfacts/
2. Facebook Newsroom (2015) Company info. Retrieved from http://newsroom.fb.com/company-info/
3. Twitter (2015) Twitter usage/company facts. Retrieved from https://about.twitter.com/company

4. Witte GG (2014) Content generation and social network interaction within academic library Facebook pages. J. Electron. Resour. Librarianship 26(2):89–100 http://doi.org/10.1080/1941126X.2014.910356
5. Emery K and Schifeling T (2015) Libraries using Twitter better: insights on engagement from food trucks. In: Creating Sustainable Community. Retrieved from http://www.ala.org/acrl/sites/ala.org.acrl/files/content/conferences/confsandpreconfs/2015/ACRL2015_A.pdf
6. MSU Communications and Brand Strategy (2013) MSU guidelines for social media. Retrieved from http://cabs.msu.edu/documents/msu-guidelines-for-social-media.pdf
7. Buck S (2012) 10 things you can fit into your 63,206-character Facebook status. Retrieved from http://mashable.com/2012/01/04/facebook-character-limit/
8. Lee K (2014) The proven ideal length of every tweet, Facebook post, and headline online. http://www.fastcompany.com/3028656/work-smart/the-proven-ideal-length-of-every-tweet-facebook-post-and-headline-online. Accessed 15 June 2015
9. Redsicker P (2014) Social photos generate more engagement. Retrieved from http://www.socialmediaexaminer.com/photos-generate-engagement-research/

Social Networks Impact on Information Consumption and Usage: e-Marefa Case

Ezz Hattab

Abstract This chapter presents social networks impact on information usage. Typically, information is being published via different channels that push information to readers. The main vehicle of information publishing is cataloging, indexing, searching, and marketing techniques. However, information that is being published via social networks is pulled and consumed by a participant (more than a reader). Information in social networks is virally published and consumed. This chapter discusses five pillars of social publishing to best utilize its features: (1) determine the nature and the structure of social networks; (2) viralize (viral-ready) the information; (3) evaluate the social information; (4) profile-oriented publishing; and (5) understand social capital as an economic value of social networks. At the end, this chapter presents a case study that embeds the concept of social networks information literacy within the e-Marefa database, which has been chosen as it includes over 252 000 records that could be viralized in social networks. The case study shows how an article could be viralized for self-publishing in an effective and efficient way. The case study found that there is a chance for an article to have one hit in 25 days ($\sim$ one month period of time) on the native platform while the same article has a chance to have 25 hits in one day via social networks.

Keywords Social publishing · Viral ready · Viralizing the content · Social capital

1 Introduction

Social networks changed the way of information production and consumption. Consequently, the role of the library is being changed to offer new features and services under an emerged term which is called Library 2.0 [1]. The concept of

This work was supported by e-Marefa

E. Hattab (✉)
Professor at Al Dar University College (The President), Dubai, UAE
e-mail: president@aldar.ac.ae

N. Taha et al. (eds.), *Social Media Shaping e-Publishing and Academia*,
DOI 10.1007/978-3-319-55354-2_2

Library 2.0 borrows features from Web 2.0 to increase interactivity and get information from the user back to the library [2]. Consumer-generated content is the major advancement of this concept.

According to studies, more than 74% of online users were moving to social networks sites in 2014 [3]. They used them as lively tools to socialize and interact in synchronous (same time) and asynchronous (different time) ways. Social networks could be defined as "an online means of communication, conveyance, collaboration and cultivation among interconnected people, communities and organizations" [4].

There are four zones of social networks: communities, publishing, entertainment, and commerce. In social communities' sites, social networks are a subject of relationships of people who share the same interest. In social publishing, sites help in publishing the content to audiences (the scope of this chapter). People can define their own content (consumer-generated content) and participate in reviewing and rating it. A good example of consumer-generated content is wikis, which are based on crowd wisdom; i.e., multiple heads better than one. In social entertainment, sites offer opportunities to share and play games. Social commerce offers new opportunities in new forms of business value such as social capital.

It is now the right time to include social networks topics within information literacy sessions. Moreover, some researchers insisted that librarians should embrace and exploit the potential of social technologies to guarantee the future of their profession [5].

This chapter recommends the basic competencies related to social networks that should be added as a subset of information literacy. Section 2 describes the nature and the structure of social networks. Section 3 handles the content itself and how to viralize it (i.e., make it viral-ready) to be socialized in an interactive way. Section 4 shows that the concept of information quality and evaluation is changed from refereed journals and citation into users' rating and ranking. Section 5 utilizes the profile features of the social networks to target the right audience and readers. Section 6 sheds light on the concept of social capital as a new value for publishers. Section 7 introduces research methods and discusses research results using the e-Marefa database. Finally, Sect. 8 concludes the work.

2 The Structure of Social Networks

The key concept of social networks is based on the small-world phenomenon with six degrees of separation that was originally set out by [6]. Every connected node (agent) is only six or fewer steps away from any other connected node in the social network as illustrated in Fig. 1.

Another interesting concept is based on the game theory that assumes an agent is a decision-making unit. This could be used to show how a social network can influence the enforcement of certain behaviors within a given structure [7].

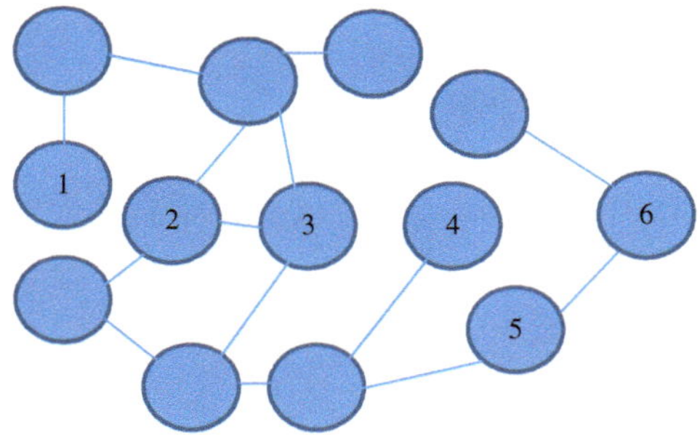

Fig. 1 Six-degree world

The underlying social structure has the following components and concepts [2].

- A *social network* is a set of socially relevant agents connected by one or more relations;
- *Agents* are members of the network;
- *Members* are connected via a relationship with each other;
- *Interactions* are behavior-based ties such as talking with each other or attending an event together;
- *Flows* are exchanges of resources, information, or influence among members of the network;
- *Content virality* is the extent to which content can be shared in social networks.

3 Content Viralization

In social networks, content is generated by consumers who are classified as follows [2]:

- Creators—create content to be shared with users;
- Conversationalists—those users who talk through social networks frequently;
- Critics—those who react to the content created by others;
- Collectors—efficient and organized users of social content;
- Joiners—people who maintain a profile on one or more social networking sites and visit the sites regularly;
- Inactives—online, but do not participate in a meaningful manner.

Using the six-degree world structure, it is easy to publish any content to any connected node (agent) in the world. To expedite the publishing process, the content should be viralized (viral-ready). Therefore, for publishers who would like to speed up the process of social publishing, it is suggested for them to adopt a psychological approach to viralize the content. Researchers found that content that includes extreme emotions (positive or negative) is more viral than other types of content [8].

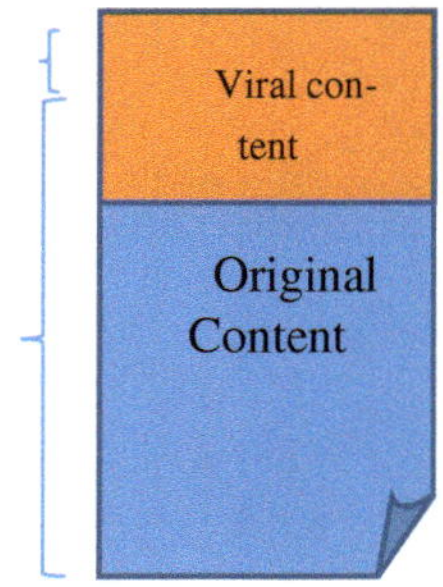

Fig. 2 Embedding viral content with the original content (viral-ready)

Thus, authors should review their content and add a metatag to viralize and make it 'viral-ready' in order to motivate people to share the content.

The following are techniques that can help to viralize the content:

Technique #1: Embed the viral content with the original content in a natural and efficient way as illustrated in Fig. 2. While there are many authors (Elites) who create exciting content that travels around the world, there are few that can successfully and consistently insert the viral message into the content.

Technique #2: To create interactive content, e.g., rating and feedback. Allow users to contribute by rating and entering their feedback and impression.

Technique #3: There are 4.5 billion 'likes' generated daily as of May 2013 which is a 67% increase from August 2012 (Source: Facebook); therefore, the competition among viral content is extremely high. To compete, viral content should make sure that keywords are embedded in the original content. Social Networks Optimization (SMO) employs tactics to increase the likelihood that others will share and promote content. SMO seeks to leverage the network effect to spread endorsements of the published content.

Technique #4: Besides the platform that publishes the content, publishers should create viral content in the most generic social networks; i.e., creating a fan page for the viral content in Facebook (Fig. 3), MySpace, Twitter, Linkedin, and Google+.

4 Social Content Evaluation

Readers trust the top ten results that appear in generic search engines or those articles that have been rated by readers regardless of the quality of this information. Moreover, in social networks there are only few influencers who maintain a huge network of people in their 'fan' pages. They are socially active and highly interconnected. Figure 4 shows the basic impact of the influencers on others; e.g., "Perez Hilton averages 220 Million Impressions and 12 Million unique readers per month" [9].

Fig. 3 e-Marefa in Facebook

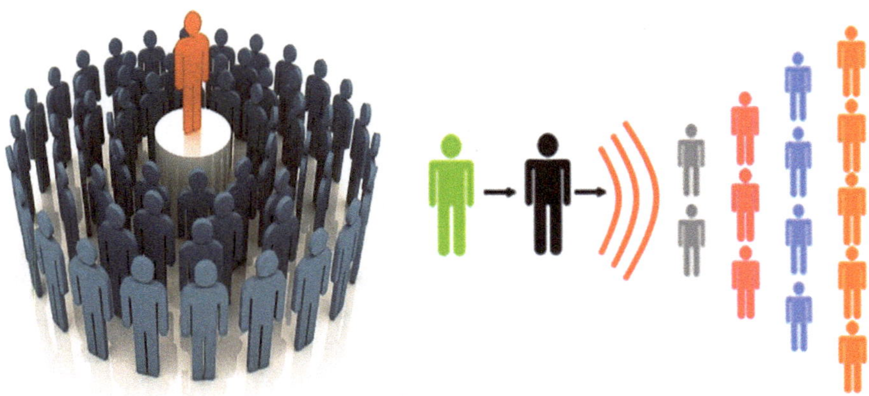

Fig. 4 The impact of the influencer

Influencers are able to change others' attitudes and behaviors. Therefore, their opinions are extremely valuable because they are competent to share information in an unbiased way.

Accordingly, it is a good strategy for publishers to recognize those influencers and share the published information with them.

5 Profile-Oriented Publishing

In social networks, all transactions are recorded as footprints or so-called 'participant prints.' This will help in understanding the behaviors of the participants who are actively engaged in content sharing. A participant print could include different profiles such as general profile, digital profile, digital usage habits, content consumption preferences, consumer content creation profile, and individual profiles.

A general profile should include basic information about the participants, demographic factors, reading patterns, the response rate to previous publishing, lifestyle data, and how readers talk about previous publishing. Publishers can collect data from prospective readers or competitors' readers as well as from current readers.

The analysis of digital usage habits will help in understanding what channels participants currently use and in what proportion. The analysis can also help answer questions such as: What sites do they surf? What kind of digital devices do they own? What are their content consumption preferences? What are participants' favored sources of information? What influences them? and What do they consider the best single source of information they can tap?

Consumer content creation profiles will answer the questions: What is created by the participants at the moment? What type of contents do they participate in? Tracking should be a standard operating procedure that gives information on what people are saying about publishing.

After analyzing the participant prints, publishers can choose the best publishing strategies, the type of the viral content that should be created, choose the keywords to publish content, and prepare the influence plan.

6 Social Capital

Social capital is defined as "the accumulated resources whose value flows to people as a result of their access to others"; (e.g., in YouTube, a view can generate $0.07). This creates new business models and motivates open data. Thus, besides subscriptions, publishers will use the social capital of their platform saying on average a published article has a certain number of views. Social capital is a formula of shared beliefs, relationships, and actions of participants' 'like' norms, behaviors, and values [2].

7 Research Method and Results

The research hypothesis is that viralized articles via social networks bring more hits and views than those articles that are being published on a platform. Consequently, the articles will contribute to increasing the overall social capital of a platform. Therefore, the chapter examined how viralized content drives social transmission and thus enhances usage and views. It studied publishing in two ways: (1) publishing via the native platform and investigating the usage report; and (2) publishing after viralizing that content on social networks and investigating the usage reports of those social networks.

In the first method, about 1500 articles have been selected from the e-Marefa database to monitor their usage and views since publishing on its native platform (i.e., e-Marefa). As an example, Fig. 6 shows the history of an article (ISN 9690) on the native platform. It has 48 hits from 16/01/2012 till 30/04/2015 (3 years and 3 months). The same article (ISN 9690) has been viralized and published on social networks. In social networks, it has 240 hits from May 2, 2015 till May 12, 2015 (10 days). Table 1 shows more examples.

This is a very interesting observation that has been generalized into 1500 articles. The ratio between the native platform and social networks was 0.03–20.5 (~ 1:625). The acceleration factor is 625, which means an article will have 625 times the number of hits on social networks compared to the native platform. In other words, it is found that there is the chance for an article to have one hit in

Table 1 More examples

Article ISN	Native platform		Social networks		Ratio
	Days	Hits	Days	Hits	
9690	1185	48	10	240	0.04:24
329463	1130	25	10	190	0.02: 19
379141	950	33	10	205	0.03:20.5
355523	1300	54	10	175	0.04:17.5
373638	1150	44	10	185	0.04:18.5
…					…
Average					0.03:18.5 (~ 1:625)

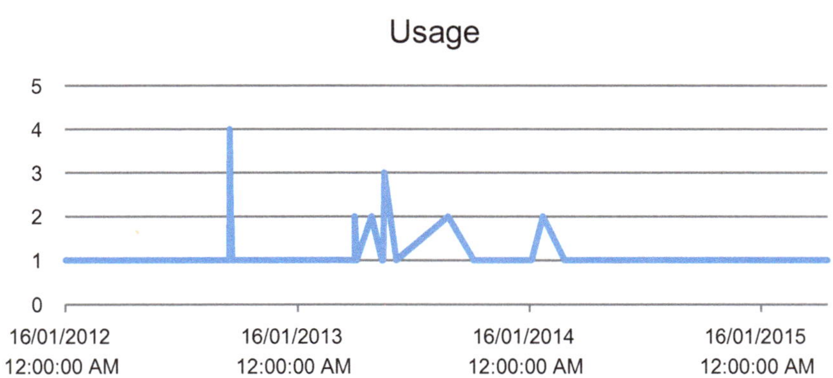

Fig. 5 A history of an article on the native platform

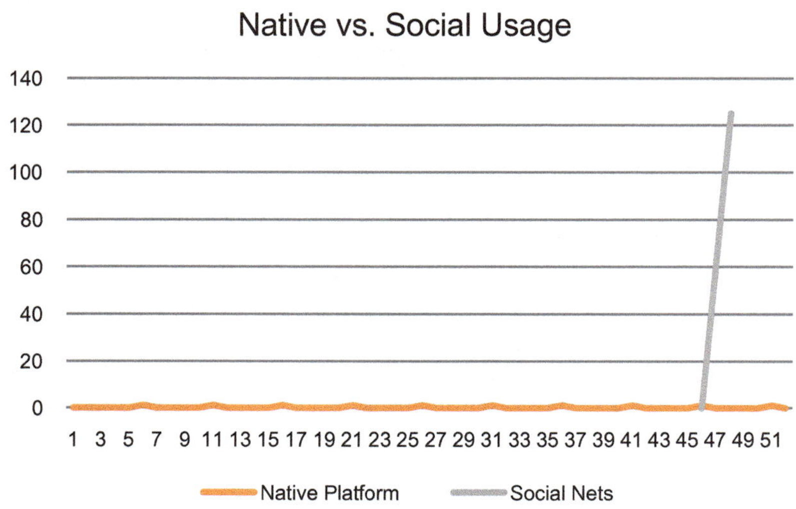

Fig. 6 Native vs. social publishing

25 days (~ one month period of time) on a native platform while the same article has a chance to have 25 hits in 1 day on social networks as depicted in Figs. 5 and 6 respectively.

8 Conclusion

Analysis of the number of hits on the native platform over 3.4 years and social networks over 10 days sheds light on the impact of social publishing using social networks over the native platform. This contributes to the hypothesis on whether viralized articles are more likely to be viewed and downloaded. The results demonstrated that viralized articles have more usage activities in social networks compared to those which are published on the native platform. These findings are consistent with the hypothesis that viralized articles bring more hits and views than those articles that are being published on the native platform. It is found that there is a possibility for an article to have one hit in 25 days (~ one month period of time) on native platforms while the same article has a possibility to have 25 hits in 1 day on social networks. For example, the usage activates are increased exponentially in a growth curve. This increase is equivalent to spending an additional 25 days for an article to have a chance of a hit on the native platform. These field results are consistent with the notion that social networks drive more usage.

Acknowledgements The author would like to acknowledge the support of e-Marefa which funded and supported this research.

References

1. Abram S (2006) Web 2.0, Library 2.0 and Librarian 2.0: preparing for the 2.0 world, SirsiDynix OneSource 2. www.imakenews.com/sirsi/e_article000505688.cfm. Accessed 9 May 2015
2. Wikipedia (2015). http://en.wikipedia.org/wiki/Library_2.0. Accessed 9 May 2015
3. Social Networking Fact Sheet (2015) http://www.pewinternet.org/fact-sheets/social-networking-fact-sheet/. Accessed 30 Apr 2015
4. Tuten T, Solomon R (2013) Social Media Marketing. Prentice Hall, Upper Saddle River
5. Daniels K et al (2011) Information literacy and Web 2.0: developing a modern media curriculum using social bookmarking and social networking tools. J. Pedagogic Develop., **1**(2)
6. Six Degrees of Separation Concept (2015) http://en.wikipedia.org/wiki/Frigyes_Karinthy. Accessed 9 May 2015
7. Cascella R, Battiti R (2007) Social Networking and Game Theory to foster Cooperation, Dipartimento di Informatica e Telecomunicazioni Universita di Trento Via Sommarive 14, 38050 Povo (TN), Italy. http://www-sop.inria.fr/members/Roberto.Cascella/publications/CB07-ENISA.pdf. Accessed 30 Apr–9 May 2015
8. Berger J, Milkman K (2012) What makes online content viral? J Mark Res 49(2):192–205
9. Hilton P (2015) http://perezhilton.com/mediakit/US/. Accessed 9 May 2015

Analysing How the Prosumption of Information in Social Media Shapes Wikipedia

Heena Siddiqi and Jawed Siddiqi

Abstract This chapter justifies the use of social media as opposed to new or digital media; within social media it argues the case for Wikipedia as an example of e-publishing. Technological, social, economic, and political perspectives on social media are briefly introduced; these are elaborated to uncover how these determinants underpin information production and consumption or more appropriately 'prosumption' in social media. This chapter applies these factors to determine how social media processes and activities as well as arrangements and organisation shape Wikipedia. It concludes that presently Wikipedia is not a commodity though it is not impossible that attempts to sell it as commodity could occur. In terms of prosumption we have shown that production is restricted to a very small minority while consumption is available to many of those with access to the appropriate digital environment. The issue of reliability of its information remains an open question. Its consumption costs are free. However, the volunteering of free labour raises the question of whether this is exploitation of labour. It contends that exploitation of labour cannot be ruled out and should be considered as an example of the way in which the whole of the technological revolution should be seen not as a break from capitalism but as an extension or intensification of late capitalism.

Keywords Social media · Wikipedia · Prosumption of information · Political economic social and technological determinants

H. Siddiqi
University of Leeds, Leeds, UK

J. Siddiqi (✉)
Sheffield Hallam University, Sheffield, UK
e-mail: J.I.Siddiqi@shu.ac.uk

N. Taha et al. (eds.), *Social Media Shaping e-Publishing and Academia*,
DOI 10.1007/978-3-319-55354-2_3

1 Why Social Media?

In the field of media and communication particularly relating to the digital era the terms 'new media', 'digital media' and 'social media' are used interchangeably; we will briefly explore these and provide the rationale for why we prefer the term 'social media'. Discussions on new media often raise the question: Why are some media considered to be 'new'? One can dismiss the answer that listing "the latest developments in media technologies and call[ing] these new" is "because the rate of change in media technologies, services platforms and uses is so rapid that any list of this sort will quickly become dated". Moreover, it has been stated that: "A paradox of new media is that the technologies that we now consider to be old were once new, and media technologies that were once new become old" [1]. A more pertinent question from our perspective is: What is new for society about the new media? According to Leivrouw and Livingstone, any approach to thinking about new media from this perspective involves: "the *artefacts and devices* that extend our ability to communicate; the communication *activities and practices* we engage into develop and use these devices; but particularly the *social arrangements and organisations* that form around these devices and practices" [2]. It is this latter point about *social arrangements* that orientates us towards the term 'social media'.

To explore further why we think the term 'social media' to be the most apt we will turn to two very early pioneers: Raymond Williams [3] and Marshall McLuhan [4], both of whom interestingly more or less ceased writing at the point when the PC was about to take off. Despite the early date of their arguments their outlook has strongly influenced approaches to understanding and thinking about media; this is because they have explored the relationships between society and technology in a way that continues to have contemporary relevance. "McLuhan's arguments are at the core of claims that 'new media change everything'" [4]; this approach argues that technology shapes society leading to what is termed in social media theory as a *technological determinism perspective*. By contrast, Lister et al. [5] claim that Williams argues that a particular technology cannot guarantee that it will shape society; this approach argues "media can only take effect through already present social processes and structures" [5]. It is for these reasons we think that the term 'social', rather than 'new' or 'digital', media fully captures the essentials we wish to pursue in this chapter.

Having explored the term 'social media' we similarly explore what we mean by and our orientation towards e-publishing or electronic publishing. Publishing in social media is simply the latest development within media whether old or new relating to the digital era and it is about mass communication. We need to remind ourselves what publishing is: in old media some obvious examples are newspapers, magazines, academic papers, books, etc. In terms of digital media or new media, their equivalents are their online counterparts and e-books. One simple but significant difference between them is the way they are produced, distributed and consumed. In old media a published magazine is produced by professionals then physically printed out and distributed through the postal system to reach the consumer often at a price. By contrast, social media allows a community to publish a magazine so that many of its members can be involved in both the production and consumption of its content and the distribution is immediate and at no cost—aside from that required for infrastructure and maintenance.

The traditional perspective on electronic publishing taken from the Wikipedia page is to point out that the process follows a traditional publishing process but differs from it in two ways: it does not include using an offset printing press to print the final product and it avoids the distribution of a physical product because the content can be made available in a variety of ways: over the Internet, on a website, in an application on a tablet or mobile device [6]. This view, in terms of social media, is limited because the producer is seen in traditional terms as the 'expert' producing content for us consumers. However, our starting point differs by focusing on what we consider is the key issue for social media: the production and consumption of the information being published; our perspective embraces the traditional view, extending it so that content is generated both by consumers and producers. In social media we are all potentially what is now termed as *prosumers* and *prosumption* is much more prevalent than separated consumption and production. Since a key aspect of both social media and electronic publishing is mass communication, Wikipedia is an ideal example of how social media processes and activities shapes e-publishing.

Section 2 briefly outlines the technological, social, economic and political perspectives that we will employ to analyse published content in social media. Section 3 expands on these perspectives to identify the technical, social, economic and political factors relating to the production, consumption and prosumption of information. Section 4 provides an account of how an analysis of these factors for information published in Wikipedia can provide a detailed commentary on how forces within social media activities and organisation can shape e-publishing.

2 Technological, Social, Economic and Political Perspectives

2.1 Technological Determinism or Social Constructivism?

As we said earlier, technological determinism is a perspective that sees technology as being responsible for shaping society. Nick Carr "in a widely read essay in the *Atlantic 2008"* [7] maintains the "long-standing tradition" by viewing technological determinism as "technology [that] is conceptualised as an external agent that acts upon and changes society". Examples of this deterministic way of thinking are [found] as far back as Ancient Greece. In *Phaedrus,* Socrates (Plato, c.370 BCE) decried the invention of the alphabet and writing as "a threat to the oral tradition of Greek society" [8]. More recently, the previously mentioned work by Carr goes as far as to claim that "Google is 'making us stupid'" and further "compared

Facebook's ability to 'enhance intelligence' with Twitter's power to 'diminish' it" [8]. Does technology so dramatically shape society?

A more reasonable variation of technological determinism is that presented by Marshall McLuhan [4] who coined the phrase the "medium is the message" meaning that technologies have characteristics that are transferred to those that use them. The sociologist Claude Fischer, well known for his study of how Americans embraced the telephone, "calls this 'impact-imprint' perspective in which technologies change history by transferring 'their essential qualities' to their users" [9]. In other words Fischer argues "a technology enters a society from outside and impacts social life". A strong interpretation of Fisher's view is that "rather than 'using' it people may be 'used by it.'; this interpretation accordingly leads us to a simplistic outlook in which "the more you use them the more they use you and the more you're influenced by them". A more "milder form of technological determinism is one in which people are seen as making and usually rational choices about which media they use for differing purposes" [8].

Social constructivism is a "perspective [that] focuses on how technologies arise from social processes" [8]; it is argued that social forces shape the way technology is used in society; therefore, not surprisingly, such a perspective views technological determinism as being inadequate for explanations, and dangerously misleading. The social historian David Nye [10] claims that "human beings, not machines are the agents of change, as men and women introduce new systems of machines that alter their life world" [8].

According to Baym the primary focus of social constructivism is how social forces influence the invention of new technologies. In his words,the proponents of social constructivism "focus on what happens during technological adoption,arguing that a wide range of social,economic,governmental,and cultural factors influence how people take up and use media"[8]. An interesting example is the Internet originally created to be used by the military as a back-up system, whereas the Internet today is used in every aspect of society by a significant proportion of the world constantly[8]. Fischer[9]illustrates factors other than social ones through the use of texting on mobile phones. It is claimed that originally text messages were hardly used amongst students in the USA, while it was more frequently used in Europe and Asia. The primary reason for this was political and economic in that regulation (political) and pricing (economic) factors inhibited its use in the USA[8].

2.2 Political and Economic Perspectives: Political Economy

In the previous section on technological and social perspectives there was revealed a degree of polar opposition, i.e. an either-or perspective, but in reality there is not such a binary divide. In terms of the political and economic perspectives it is more apt to think of them in complementary terms as they are inextricably linked. Indeed Ha-Joon Chang [11] in his popular book on economics makes the point that traditional economics was simply political economy and we concur and follow this view; therefore for us political economy draws upon economics and political science to explain how institutions, the state and the economic system: capitalist, socialist or mixed, influence each other. From this perspective we briefly characterise capitalism and socialism. Capitalism is an economic system based on private ownership of the means of production and the creation of goods and services for profit. Politically, it is a system based on private property rights, including the private ownership of resources or capital, with economic decisions made largely through the operation of a free market. Therefore, information is simply a commodity. By contrast, socialism from a Marxist perspective is an intermediate phase of social development between capitalism and full communism in which the state has control of the means of production. The latter involves the people holding the resources collectively and the state withers away. Information is therefore collectively created and owned.

From the above we can see that information can either be privately or collectively owned. In the former case, information is a commodity which means the information is restricted, produced by a few, owned by a few, and involves costs for production and consumption; in the latter case, it is available to everybody, produced by everybody, owned by everybody, and involves no cost in the production or consumption. It is in the spirit of these terms that we explicate the technological, social, economic and political determinants of social media in the next section and will in Sect. 4 apply them to analyse how social media arrangements and organisation is shaping e-publishing in the form of Wikipedia.

3 Explicating the Underpinning Determinants of Social Media

3.1 Internet, World Wide Web and Wikipedia: The Tensions

In the 1960s the Governments of the United States, the UK and France commissioned research and development to build a robust, fault-tolerant communication system via computer networks or what is now termed the Internet [12]. Barbrook [13] claims that despite the Net being created for the US Military and the Pentagon trying to restrict its use exclusively for official military business, "it soon became obvious that the Net could only be successfully developed by letting its users build the system for themselves". So we can see from the outset that there was a tension between those that wanted an open and free for all to use product and those that wanted the product to be highly restricted. The founders of the World Wide Web challenged this tension involved in the construction of the Internet, upon which the worldwide web was constructed from the outset. In contrast to the military the founders of the World Wide Web sought its use to promote the distribution of information without barriers and to be freely available to all. Indeed Tim

Berners-Lee, often considered to be the inventor of the Web, was very clear what it was originally designed for and what its future use should be:

"The World Wide Web was designed originally as an interactive world of shared information through which people could communicate with each other and with machines…In the future we look towards the web becoming a tool for even smaller groups, families, and personal information systems" [14].

In the context of Web 2.0, Lister et al. [15] discuss the "tensions between the creative, open source practices of web media and the economic and commercial forces with which they react"; they illustrate through the case of Tim O'Reilly, a media consultant working for a company organising media trade conferences, who 'sold' the notion of Web 2.0 as something that encourages "co-creativity, participation and openness, presented by softwares (sic) that support, for example, wiki based ways of creating and accessing knowledge, social networking sites, blogging, tagging and 'mashups'". O'Reilly expresses the transition of Web 1.0 to Web 2.0 in highly technological terms as well as emphasising openess and participation; however, the production and consumption of information was largely controlled by an external authority—the owner—even though it had the potential to be controlled by the consumer or users themselves. In short Lister et al. [15] perceptively points out that some saw the Internet as "marketing slogan from its inception [having]… a clear economic goal".

A key figure contributing to this discussion was Richard Stallman, a computer programmer and founder of the Free Software Foundation, who actively campaigns for software to be freely available. He campaigns for software to be easily available in a form that enables all users to scrutinise, modify, and distribute it. In 1999 Stallman invited the public at large to contribute articles to build up a free online encyclopaedia that resulted in GNUPedia that was eventually retired because of the success of Wikipedia [16]. Therefore, the origin of Wikipedia can be traced to the influence of Stallman. Indeed on the Wikipedia page in the history section there is an acknowledgment to that effect. In fact the original version of Wikipedia was Nupedia, a free online English language encyclopaedia. Its content was contributed and reviewed by experts whose license was switched to a Free Documentation license of the sort urged by Richard Stallman. Jimmy Wales had the idea of producing and consuming content by the public in the spirit of Richard Stallman whereas Larry Sanger had the idea of using the notion of a Wiki to create Wikipedia [17].

3.2 Prosumer Capitalism

Up to now we have focused on how technological and social forces have enabled information to be collectively gathered. We now move on to discuss the concept of information as a commodity from a political and economic perspective. This necessitates focusing on production and consumption but particularly on the notion of 'prosumtion', previously mentioned, as well as the corresponding agent of prosumption—the*prosumer*. One key work that looks at prosumption particularly in relation to information from an economic perspective is by Ritzer and Jurgenson [18], whose work focuses on *prosumer* capitalism; this is different from a traditional capitalist system based on the separation of production and consumption. Indeed, they argue that Marx focused too much on production at the expense of consumption and Baudrillard later broke with this tradition and realized the "centrality of consumption". However, for Ritzer and Jurgenson prosumer capitalism has become central to the understanding of information as a commodity given the arrival of social media.

Ritzer and Jurgenson traced the origin of their perspective to the work of Toffler [19], in the 80s, who "argued that prosumption was predominant in pre-industrial societies;" and had talked about how "society is moving away from the aberrant separation of production and consumption and towards a 'third wave' that, in part, signals their reintegration in 'the rise of the prosumer'" [18]. It is interesting to note at this point how Toffler's insight into the notion of a *prosumer* preceded the social media age.

Amongst the key differences of prosumer capitalism compared to traditional capitalism, is the fact that that content is not scarce and is created but not by paid employees. Moreover, the cost of hosting massive amounts of digital content is significantly shrinking and the ever-increasing volume of users creating content on social media sites rapidly leads to products or commodities that are freely available in abundance. Similarly, whereas traditional capitalism aims to be highly efficient—meaning minimising cost and maximising profit; the focus of prosumer capitalism is quality—meaning creation of effective products and services [18].

Ritzer and Jurgenson's view of digital prosumer capitalism is distinct in these major ways:

- Difficulty in controlling prosumers as compared to producers or consumers;
- Exploitation of prosumers is less clear-cut;
- There is a distinct economic system emerging where services are free and prosumers are not paid for their work;
- Abundance rather than scarcity of content;
- Effectiveness of content rather than cost-efficient production.

In Summary, therefore prosumer capitialism appears to challenge the notion of information as a commodity

3.3 *Information as a Gift or Commodity?*

Barbrook [13] claims to be one of the earliest to point out from an economic perspective that the two conflicting ideologies of capitalism, in which information is produced and consumed as a commodity; and socialism, in which information is produced and consumed for the common good of all, could co-exist. Both communities were fascinated by developments in technology and despite their irreconcilable goals believed that technological determinism would/could support and be used exclusively for one or the other's economic goal. He strongly objected to this simple binary divide position and asserted that both modes of production and consumption, or as we call it *prosumption,* could exist side by side. In Barbrook's words: "On the Net, the same piece of information could exist both as a commodity and a gift". He cites the well known example of free 'illegal' downloading of files. The "movie and music industries have forced the leading file sharing services to limit unauthorized copying by their users. But as soon as one threat is seen off, another arises" [13].

The exchange of information between academics who are spread across the world is an obvious example of what Barbrook terms a 'gift economy'. Academics acquire intellectual respect from each other through citations in articles and other forms of public acknowledgement. Scientists therefore obtain personal recognition for their individual efforts by openly collaborating with each other through the academic gift economy. Although research is being increasingly commercialised, the giving away of findings remains the most efficient method of solving common problems within a particular scientific discipline. Indeed this form of exchange of information has expanded far beyond academia. Now dedicated hobbyists, enthusiastic practitioners to the general public, are contributing their collective knowledge and making it accessible to all those online. The majority on the Internet are able to receive far more than they could individually contribute. So from Barbrook's perspective, the exchange of information on Wikipedia remains predominantly a gift economy because numerous individuals freely provide vast amounts of information accessible to all.

We briefly explore the role of information from a political perspective through a key work in social media by Terranova [20] who focuses on free labour in the digital era. Free labour is undervalued in capitalist societies, but at the same time he states that: "the internet is animated by cultural and technical labour through and through, a continuous production of value that is completely immanent to the flows of the network society at large". His work challenges the work by Ritzer and Jurgenson that largely promotes the benefits of free labour. He cites a number of examples where there was a "necessary backlash against the glamorization of digital labor"; indeed he thinks it is simply a continuity of "the modern sweatshop and points to the increasing degradation of knowledge work". Terranova [20] explores free labour in relation to the digital economy but not simply as "the familiar logic of capitalist exploitation" but "is rather a mutation that is totally immanent to late capitalism, not so much a break as an intensification, and therefore a mutation, of a widespread cultural and economic logic".

4 Social Media Shaping E-publishing

The Community of Wikipedia contributors are all volunteers and its size has grown exponentially showing that social media is shaping the online publishing of information. Clearly a massive amount of free labour has gone into the production of its content. Some interesting data for 2011 is available on the Wikipedia Community page. Worldwide across all language editions there were approximately 31.7 million registered user accounts, of which only around 270 000 were 'active' making at least one edit every month meaning, therefore, that less than 1% (0.85) were active contributors. The corresponding figures in terms of activity for the English Wikipedia is that about 0.4% are active though about half of those spend at least one hour a day editing, and a fifth spend more than three hours a day [21].

A Wikipedia Editor survey conducted in 2011 found that the most frequent (60% or more) motivation for of the contributors volunteering was: to share information and expertise; information should be free; and it's fun. The most frequent reason for stopping contributing was: being derided by experts; having your edits reversed without explanation; or articles deleted. This sense of sharing information freely and the sense of self-satisfaction has been replicated by other studies, all available at [21]. Wikipedia is therefore a prime example of a social media application or even a phenomenon where information is published collectively both by producers and consumers. It is clearly shaping e-publishing or as Lister concisely sums up, Wikipedia is " the prototypical model of an open source user generated knowledge world" [15].

On Wikipedia it appears that in principle there is a huge volume of individual prosumers working together to produce content that is timely and accurate. However, let us consider the activity from a social perspective, namely the participation of those contributing. We can see that those that are active participants are a very small fraction of those that are registered. However, the picture gets even more interesting when one unpacks what it means to contribute to editing and providing content. According to Swartz, who looked at those that produce content from those that simply edit content, his findings replicated the results found on the Wikipedia page about editing. He also investigated the common perception that content is produced "by thousands and thousands of individual contributors each adding a little bit of content and out of this emerges a coherent body of work"; and Wales' counter claim that it was "a community … a dedicated group of a few hundred volunteers" where "I know all of them and they all know each other". He found on the few pages that he monitored that often the original contributors of the text of the article made very few edits and that the vast majority were done by registered users; also most of the edits "were *small changes*: people fixing typos, formatting, links, categories, and so on, making the article a little nicer but not adding much in the way of substance". A few of the editors added a "smaller number [which] were *genuine additions*: a couple sentences or even paragraphs of new information added to the page" [22]. So much for Wales' claim that "it's going to be part of everyday life – creating and sharing media will be a thing that normal people will do all the time, everyday, and it doesn't seem strange" [15]. So it would appear that while those producing content may be a larger pool, the vast majority of contributors are simply editing. Further evidence of the narrowness in participation comes from Simonite. "The volunteer workforce that built the project's flagship, the English language Wikipedia—and must defend it against vandalism, hoaxes, and manipulation—has shrunk by more than a third since 2007 and is still shrinking"

[23]. In considering the gender of contributors, Collier and Bear report that less than 15% of contributors are female. Interestingly the reason for them to not contribute is due to: the high level of conflict involved in the editing, debating, and defending processes; lower confidence in their expertise and in the value of their contribution; they prefer to share and collaborate rather than delete and change other's work—that is, they don't feel comfortable editing [24].

Barbrook makes the assertion that: "Most internet users collaborate with each other without the direct mediation of money or politics, unconcerned about copyright they give and receive information without thought or payment" [13]. These viewpoints embrace the second and third distinctive characteristics of prosumer capitalism (c.f. p. 7). Therefore, it appears that there is no commercial exploitation and there is a new economic system emerging; leading us to think about the political and economic dimensions of how social media shapes Wikipedia.

Referring to the first characteristic of prosumer capitalism (c.f. p. 7), applied to Wikipedia it does not tally with the evidence on the editing of contributions. It appears that there is a cabal of predominantly male contributors constantly and in large volume controlling the content often with minor revisions that do not add to the content; additionally, certain sites are locked and therefore cannot be changed. All this is far from it being difficult to control prosumers because, as the research shows, the most popular reasons for not contributing are excessive editing and being derided by so-called experts. Turning to the last two characteristics about abundance and effectiveness of content, there is certainly an abundance of content. An early study cited on the Wikipedia page on the reliability of Wikipedia in the journal *Nature* said that in 2005, Wikipedia's scientific articles came close to the level of accuracy in *Encyclopedia Britannica* and numerous others on the same page suggest similar results [17]. However, closer scrutiny of all these results indicate that the sample sizes are far too small to make claims about its accuracy and reliability. Indeed Wikipedia's own article on 'Controversies in Wikipedia' enumerates numerous examples of mistakes found. Perhaps one the most serious mistakes in media terms was when Lord Justice Leveson, writing on British press standards, had used the Wikipedia article on the *Independent* newspaper as his source; however, without realising that it had been 'vandalised'. From the small amount of evidence available, the accuracy of the information remains an open question. Taking the approach adopted by many academics that it should be avoided is probably based on the lack of peer evaluation, which is understandable but perhaps too harsh; nevertheless, to use it as the sole source for information is not recommended.

In conclusion returning to our original criteria which are based on social, political, and economic perspectives of social media, information can either be privately or collectively owned (i.e. a commodity) meaning it is restricted, produced by a few, owned by a few, and involves costs in production and consumption; or from a collective perspective it is available to everybody, produced by everybody, owned by everybody, and no cost in the production or consumption. Specifically in the case of Wikipedia it is clearly not a commodity and its consumption costs are nil. In terms of prosumption we have shown that the production is restricted to a very small minority, while the consumption is available to the many with access to the appropriate digital environment. In terms of ownership Wikipedia is not owned by its producers and consumers. It is possible it could be sold as a commodity, as unlikely and difficult as that may presently appear to its advocates.

To answer the question as to whether workers have been exploited, Terranova's analysis applied to social media in general does confirm the exploitation of labour. His work views the whole of the technological revolution as not a break from capitalism but as an extension or intensification of late capitalism; a view that very much accords with the direction that we think needs further investigation. This viewpoint provides a future direction in which to pursue the role of technology in a post-capitalist society ranging from the early classics of Mandel's *Late Capitalism* [25] and Jameson's *Postmodernism, or The Cultural Logic of Late Capitalism* [26] to the recent contributions of Mason's *Post Capitalism: A Guide To Our Future* [27] and Srnicek and Williams' *Inventing the Future: Post-capitalism and a World Without Work* [28].

References

1. Flew T (2014) Introduction to New Media. In: Flew T (ed) New Media, 4th edn. Oxford University Press, South Melbourne, pp 2–17
2. Leivrouw L, Livingstone S (2006) The Handbook of New Media, Student Edition
3. Williams R (1958) Culture and Society. Chatto and Windus, London
4. McLuhan M et al (1967) The medium is the message. Bantam, New York
5. Lister M, Dovey J, Giddens S, Grant I, Kelly K (2009) New media: determining or determined? New Media a critica Introduction, 2nd edn. Routledge, Abingdon, pp 9–13
6. Wikipedia, Electronic Publishing, https://en.wikipedia.org/wiki/Electronic_publishing
7. Carr N (2008) Is Google Making Us Stupid? The Atlantic, July/August http://www.theatlantic.com/magazine/archive/2008/07/is-google-making-us-stupid/306868/
8. Baym N (2015) Making new media make sense. Personal Connections in the Digital Age, 2nd edn. Polity Press, Cambridge, pp 24–56
9. Fischer C (1992) America Calling: A Social History of the Telephone to 1940. University of California Press, Berkeley
10. Nye DE (1997) Shaping communication networks: Telegraph, telephone, computer. Soc Res, 1067–1091
11. Ha-Joon C (2014) Economics: The User Guide, Bloomsbury Press, New York
12. Wikipedia, Internet https://en.wikipedia.org/wiki/Internet
13. Barbrook R (1998) The high-tech gift economy. First Monday, 3(12). Accessed 13 Sept 2015
14. Berners-Lee T (1996) The World Wide Web: Past, Present and Future https://www.w3.org/People/Berners-Lee/1996/ppf.html
15. Lister M, Dovey J, Giddens S, Grant I, Kelly K (2009) Wiki worlds and web 2.0. In: New Media: A Critical Introduction. 2nd ed. Abingdon: Routledge, pp. 204–209
16. Stallman R (2016) The Free Universal Encyclopedia and Learning Resource. Accessed Jan. 2016
17. Wikipedia, Wikipedia https://en.wikipedia.org/wiki/Wikipedia
18. Ritzer G, Jurgenson N (2010) Production, consumption, prosumption: the nature of capitalism in the age of the digital 'prosumer'. J Consum. Culture. 10(1):13–36
19. Toffler A (1980) The Third Wave. Bantam Books, New York

20. Terranova T (2000) Free labour: producing culture for the digital economy. Soc Text 18 (2):33–58
21. Wikipedia, Wikipedia Community. https://enwikipedia.org/wiki/Wikepedia_community
22. Swartz A http://www.aaronsw.com/2002/whowriteswikipedia/swartz2006perspective
23. Simonite T (2013) The decline of Wikipedia. Technology Review 116(6):50–56
24. Collier B, Bear J (2012) Conflict, criticism, or confidence: an empirical examination of the gender gap in wikipedia contributions. In: Proceedings of the ACM 2012 conference on computer supported cooperative work, pp 383–392
25. Mandel E (1975) Late Capitalism, trans. Joris De Bres, New York
26. Jameson F (1993) Postmodernism, or The Cultural Logic of Late Capitalism. A Reader, Postmodernism
27. Mason P (2015) Post Capitalism: A Guide To Our Future. Allen Lane, London
28. Srnicek N, Williams A (2015) Inventing the Future: Post-capitalism and a World Without Work. Verso Books, London

Part II
Social Media and E-Learning

Social media networks are playing an important role in e-learning, as they increase human relations between members of the community. Also, they are one of the most popular communication mediums due to their simplicity. The globe has become a small village where anything can be reached from anywhere at any time, by only pressing a few buttons on your personal computer or cell phone. Social Media Networks (SMNs) are software designed by professionals in order to enable people to communicate and interact about any topic. They also can be described as a group of people; usually called 'friends', who are connected with each other to exchange their ideas, views, and thoughts about any topic. Popular SMNs such as Facebook, Twitter, and others attracted educational institutions to take advantage of them. They have been used to provide new learning styles that are based on sharing learning resources and a new method of communication; it has even been claimed that they actually replaced the old style, which was based on a one-way dialogue. So, IT professionals have found that SNMs provide a suitable environment for modern learning systems which meet learners' needs and expectations and keep pace with the technological revolution.

The wide spread of new technologies such as smart phones made the ability of using SMNs even more popular and made integrating their usage with learning easier, simpler, more attractive, and fun. Many SMN techniques can be employed here such as e-blogs, Facebook groups, and using Twitter to check what is written about something. In addition, they give a broad horizon for exchanging experiences and experiments between experts; they can be used to raise the innovation and creativity of both students and instructors. However, the lack of sufficient awareness of using these networks may be reflected negatively on the level of interaction between students and the academic level of the student, as some groups that are shown as ostensibly positive conceal negative content that is difficult to be discovered by naive students.

We present in this part of the book four new research chapters. The first chapter examines the role of social networks in increasing activity of e-learning. The authors present a survey of social networks' role in increasing the activity of e-learning by assessing the risks and advantages of using these networks, in addition to the direct and indirect influence of the efficiency of e-learning. Fuzzy logic systems have been used to analyze a set of questionnaires distributed among students of Avicenna Center in Erbil-Kurdistan Region-Iraq for e-learning. The results showed that there is, in the first steps, a negative influence of social networks on e-learning, but that, gradually, this influence becomes apparently positive and more active.

The second chapter explores the use of IPython for teaching web scraping where the authors employed IPython to support educators in teaching the fundamentals of web scraping. The authors identified providing detailed labs as free online resources together with model answers as the main contribution of this chapter.

The author of the third chapter examines the role of social network sites in connecting students with learning and academic activities. This case study investigated the use of SNS among undergraduate students in an attempt to support their learning and academic activities. The results revealed that all students used at least one social network site. The results also showed how students connect for the purpose of learning or for any other academic activity. Recommendations are drawn from the findings regarding the use of SNS among students and the role that academics may play to further encourage the phenomenon.

The fourth chapter is an investigation of social media e-publishing among Jordanian university students. The author of this study investigated SNS and e-publishing usage among undergraduate students at the University of Jordan. Results indicated a widespread usage of SNS and a strong attachment to SNS in general such as Facebook and to less popular ones such as Twitter, Instagram and Snapchat; they are generally used to connect people from near and far. The respondents emphasized SNS as a means of socialization more than a learning medium, so sharing and exchanging information was the norm using e-publishing such as blogs, e-books, e-journals, and online newspapers, while digital library usage was relegated to a minor position. Also, the respondents fear privacy issues, security risks and identity theft.

Rizik Al-Sayyed

The Role of Social Networks in Increasing the Activity of E-learning

Thabit Hassan Thabit and Yaser Abdul Aali Jasim

Abstract The Information Technology (IT) revolution in communications and social networks showed a wide spreading and huge development, which led to use of this technology in many aspects of everyday life. As a result, a lot of functions concerned with e-systems have appeared and been transformed from a classical version into the e-version. Therefore, e-learning was one of the systems which resulted from this technology. This chapter presents a survey of social networks' role in increasing the activity of e-learning by assessing the risks and advantages of using these networks; the direct and indirect influences of the efficiency of e-learning are also discussed. Fuzzy logic systems have been used to analyze a set of questionnaires distributed among students of *Avicenna Center* in Erbil, Kurdistan region, Iraq for e-learning. The results show that there is, in the first steps, a negative influence of social networks one-learning; gradually, however, this influence becomes apparently positive and more active.

Keywords E-learning · Social networks · Fuzzy logic · Information Technology (IT)

1 Introduction

Social media has become a big part of our daily lives. Computers are increasingly used to communicate and interact with others. The Internet and its advantages of connectivity enable e-learning to be used for a variety of applications. The most common uses of the Internet include e-mail communication, discussion forums, as well as real-time chat rooms and audio/video conferencing. By communicating

T.H. Thabit (✉) · Y.A.A. Jasim
Erbil, Iraq
e-mail: thabit.acc@gmail.com

Y.A.A. Jasim
e-mail: yaser.a.jasim@gmail.com

N. Taha et al. (eds.), *Social Media Shaping e-Publishing and Academia*,
DOI 10.1007/978-3-319-55354-2_4

through computers and over the Internet, online communities emerge. The use of social network applications in e-learning courses fosters the development of online communities. Discussion boards and other internet applications offer a large amount of data. The analysis of this can help us to understand communities.

2 E-learning

2.1 The Definition

E-learning is the use of electronic media, educational technology, and Information and Communication Technologies (ICT) in education [1]. It includes numerous types of media that deliver text, audio, images, animation, and streaming video, and includes technology applications and processes such as audio or video tape, satellite TV, CD-ROM, and computer-based learning, as well as local intranet/extranet and web-based learning. Information and communication systems, whether free-standing or based on either local networks or the Internet in networked learning, underlie many e-learning processes [2].

E-learning can be defined as "learning that is supported by information and communications technologies". The characteristics of e-learning are that there is a physical distance between the students and teachers, and usually electronic technologies are used for the delivery of the material [3].

2.2 Historical Background

By the 1990s, multimedia development brought about substantial improvements in the quality of educational programs and software. The development and dissemination of e-learning was greatly enhanced by the development of the World Wide Web (WWW), because its software was able to incorporate internet sources and applications as well as resource tools. Technology and learning continued to improve with respect to the rapid developments associated with improvements to the learning environment. Furthermore, e-learning is developed by effecting changes to the structure of those technologies [4].

E-learning has attracted the attention of educational institutions, especially with regard to adapting it to the classroom environment [5]. E-learning offers a number of educational advantages; for example, its flexibility is considered to be a contemporary approach that supports teaching and the learning environment. In addition, e-learning supports professional development and best practice via the use of internet tools that provide 'rich-technology' for classroom activities [6].

2.3 Benefit and Drawback of E-learning

E-learning is very effective in higher education if it is conducted correctly. It has been argued that e-learning has the advantage of enabling learners and academics to improve their skills and provide channels for communication. The introduction of e-learning offers a chance to innovate the learning system. Moreover, it is claimed that e-learning has been used very advantageously in higher education in terms of enabling learners to become self-directed learners [7].

Consonant with that, e-learning applications support individual learning experiences and interaction, encourage critical thinking, improve communication between learners and instructors, develop cooperative learning, and facilitate the learning environment [8].

E-learning provides learners with rich opportunities to connect to appropriate learning experiences, which offers them the opportunity to engage and experience a variety of diverse techniques and thus receive different supports for their learning and so develop their understanding [7].

There is considerable scope for the use of e-learning in education. There are four main reasons for e-learning initiatives in higher education [8]:

1. To develop the value of learning.
2. To reduce the cost of education.
3. To develop accessibility for teaching and training purposes.
4. To improve the impact value of education.

In addition, some scholars expanded the vision by describing the benefits of e-learning by determining four R's that could assist learners [7].

- Relationship—learners' engagements with e-learning tools provide a chance for collaborative activities, e.g. shared websites (blog and Wiki).
- Reflection—it is required and needed when completing actions via e-learning. Learners are able to develop their reflective skills in terms of academic aptitude and commitment.
- Resourcefulness—utilizing e-learning provides skills by dealing with different resources, e.g. data based and searching skills. In addition, learners could gain knowledge via experience and communicate with different activities though internet interactions.
- Resilience—because of the above three points, there is an opportunity to provide a resilient environment where learners have to attain a high level of interactivity thus developing time management skills.

Similar advantages have been addressed by Rosenberg (2001). He said that lower costs together with flexibility of time makes e-learning efficient. He continues to argue in more detail that time is not restricted for doing tasks via e-learning resources. For example, it is not disrupted by breaks, conversations, class rules, etc. Another point is that the learners are able to move from one task to another. There is a tendency for learners to exceed any information that they already know.

The learner, therefore, is free of the negative effects of being in a classroom. Some learners need more time to achieve some tasks and their successful completion will improve a learner's experience and motivation.

There is agreement that utilizing e-learning within the learning environment improves the quality of education systems by integrating web applications, such as storyboards and the blackboard portals, via the Internet. There is evidence that the learning environment is also enhanced because it gains high performance, skills, and efficiency [9] and it seems that higher education has increased the use of e-learning, especially through the use of the new internet services [10].

There is a need to benefit from the experiences that are encountered when using e-learning applications. Researchers have noticed a marked gap between what is currently perceived as good implementation with what actually occurs in practice [11] and what educational institutions do to achieve success.

3 The Social Network

3.1 Definition

Social networks are a social structure of nodes that represent individuals (or organizations) and the relationships between them within a certain domain. The strength of relationships and trust among nodes (members) are used to construct the social networks. Scrutiny of the ways in which these nodes are connected has resulted in the identification of varying types of ties between nodes [12].

A social network is defined by some researchers as a web-based service which allows members to build a public or semi-public profile embodied in a bounded system, explain things to a list of other individuals with whom they share a connection, and present and convert their list of connections and those made by others included in the system. The nature and nomenclature of these connections may vary from site to site [13].

3.2 Historical Background

At the end of nineteenth century, some scholars predicted the idea of social networks in their theories and research about social groups.

According to Tönnies, social groups can exist as private and direct social links that either connect persons who share values and confidence or are impersonal, formal, and tactical social connections. On the other hand, Durkheim argued a collective demonstration of social facts, given that when interacting individuals constitute the social phenomena, it will raise a fact in the properties of individual actors. Georg Simmel, at the beginning of twentieth century, pointed to the nature of networks and the impact of network expansion on interaction, and tested the probability of interaction in loosely bound networks rather than groups [14].

In the 1930s, major progress can be noticed by several groups in psychology, anthropology, and mathematics working independently. In psychology, Moreno began systematic recording and analysis of social interaction in small groups, especially classrooms and work groups. In anthropology, a group of social anthropologists associated with Gluckman and the Manchester School, including Barnes, Mitchell and Spillius, are often credited with performing some of the first fieldwork from which network analyses were performed, investigating community networks in a number of countries. Synchronously, British anthropologist Nadel codified a theory of social structure that was influential in later network analysis. In sociology, Parsons set the stage for taking a relational approach to understanding social structure. Later, the sociologist Blau provided a strong motive to analyze the relational connections of social groups with social exchange theory. After more than four decades, a growing number of researchers worked to merge the different tracks and traditions [15].

3.3 Advantages and Disadvantages

Nowadays, a social network is a very global component and has significant impact and influence on the social and business lives of people. As with any term that appears, a social network will face different opinions that describe the advantages and disadvantages of it. Hence, the advantages and disadvantages are mentioned as follows [16]:

(1) The Advantages:

1. Helps users to keep in touch with colleagues, relatives, friends, and partners from a distance.
2. Promotes products and services perfectly.
3. Supports people to present themselves online.
4. A good platform for doing charity business.
5. Powerful platform to find job vacancies.
6. Can be used for detecting cases of crime.
7. Increases political will for bodies.
8. Helps researchers to find new terms and concepts in different fields for scientific research.

(2) The Disadvantages:

1. Wastes a lot of individuals' time and holds them back from communicating in other important activities.
2. Reduces real human activities such as wishing someone happy birthday by posting it online instead of doing personally or by phone.

3. Creates a wide gap between people who have access to the Internet and people who do not.
4. Affects the privacy of users.
5. Affects public policy and causes a lot of environmental changes.
6. Can become a way to destabilize the government by publishing bad posts.
7. Can be used to promote crime.
8. Can be a reason to ruin the structure of a particular language.

4 The Relationship Between Social Network and E-learning

There are four common activities that are used in the learning process [17]:

- Create content information: users can generate concepts, assign their work publicly, and allow them to develop the content by sharing it with many learning communities.
- Share information: users are able to enhance and widen the content gradually.
- Interactive: users can be left to their comments, reviews, and ratings on the discussion boards that will lead to active discussion.
- Social partnership: users can communicate among themselves by active social cooperation to resolve a particular issue through a social network.

5 The Use of Social Media as E-learning Platforms

Social media is substantially a virtual texture that consists of individuals, communities, groups or organizations with similar interests, visions, attitudes, ethical values, lifestyles, and friendships and in the domain of e-learning. This virtual texture can be used in many different ways and by a number of tools such as [18]:

Facebook
This social networking website can be very useful for instructors by creating a closed or open group for sharing data, information, tests, quizzes, materials, or even an entire page on a specific course. On the other hand, students can talk about various course-related issues, ask questions, or post information or anything else.

Twitter
The instructor can use Twitter in e-learning as a backchannel to connect learning communities like small classrooms over a specific concept, topic, term, or event, by

creating an account and communicate using private #hashtags, upload pictures and share related links.

LinkedIn
This purely professional social network can be extremely useful in e-learning. Many instructors share views, problems, developments, and how-to tips; hence, it will be easy for educators, students, or other users to gain benefits from them, and to share their opinion about many subjects.

Google Plus
E-learning professionals believe that Google Plus is going to be the most popular social media that is used as a learning platform. The reasons for this are that both learners and facilitators are getting less distracted versus Facebook and Twitter; also most students do not like to use their social networks for their studies.

YouTube
This website can be the best resource for e-learning, because it is free, available, can be used to support the class or lecture with extra materials or examples, and the video content can be rated by the students easily.

6 Practical Part

For the purpose of this study, 50 questionnaires were prepared by the researchers and distributed to students that come to the Avicenna Center in Erbil. The questionnaire had two parts; the first part was about e-learning, and the second part was about the social network. After 3 months the same questionnaires were distributed again to the same sample of students.

The researchers processed the data of the 100 questionnaires and analyzed it by Fuzzy logic tools and using Matlab 10.

7 The Questionnaire

The questionnaire had two parts with 10 questions in each, as shown in Tables 1 and 2.

The results of above questionnaire for the first 50 questionnaires (at the beginning of the study) were processed and analyzed using fuzzy logic tools; the results of the analysis are shown in Table 3.

Figures 1 and 2 show the results that were analyzed for the first 50 questionnaires in linear charts.

The results of the second 50 questionnaires (at the end of the study) were analyzed and processed using fuzzy logic tools; the results are shown in Table 4.

Figures 3 and 4 show the analyzed results of the second 50 questionnaires in linear charts.

Table 1 The first part of the questionnaire

S	Question	Code
1	The duration of attending the e-learning lectures	Q1
2	The number of e-learning lectures attended	Q2
3	The type of media used	Q3
4	The number of hours attending e-learning lectures virtually at home	Q4
5	The technique of using e-mail	Q5
6	The number of subjects of e-learning lectures attended	Q6
7	The benefit of using e-learning	Q7
8	The opinion of digital reading	Q8
9	The sending or receiving of lectures among students by e-mail	Q9
10	The type of device used (laptop, desktop, smart phone, tablet)	Q10

Table 2 The second part of the questionnaire

S	Question	Code
1	The duration of using social network	I1
2	The number of login hours	I2
3	The number of browsing hours	I3
4	The sending or receiving of lectures among students by social media	I4
5	The technique of using e-mail	I5
6	The number of hours using social media	I6
7	The benefit of using social media	I7
8	The number of scientific groups on social network	I8
9	The type of pages on social network	I9
10	The activity on social network	I10

Table 3 The analyzed results of the first and second parts of the questionnaires

S	Q	%	I	%
1	Q1	12	I1	22
2	Q2	14	I2	30
3	Q3	22	I3	44
4	Q4	15	I4	27
5	Q5	10	I5	33
6	Q6	25	I6	41
7	Q7	30	I7	37
8	Q8	22	I8	32
9	Q9	26	I9	28
10	Q10	16	I10	29

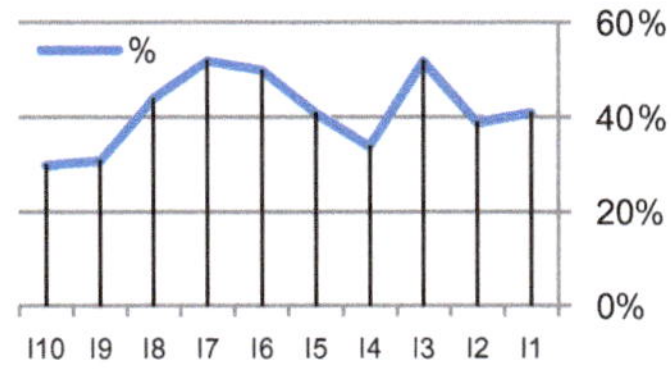

Fig. 1 The linear chart for the first part of the questionnaire

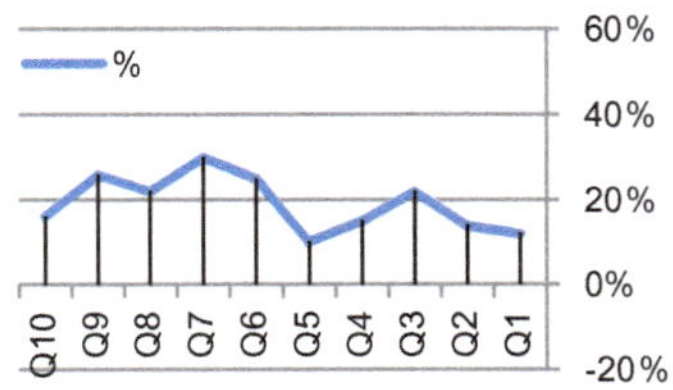

Fig. 2 The linear chart for the second part of the questionnaire

Table 4 The analyzed results of first and second parts of the questionnaires (at the end of the study)

S	Q	%	I	%
1	Q1	14	I1	41
2	Q2	16	I2	39
3	Q3	25	I3	52
4	Q4	18	I4	34
5	Q5	13	I5	41
6	Q6	28	I6	50
7	Q7	33	I7	52
8	Q8	28	I8	44
9	Q9	31	I9	31
10	Q10	21	I10	30

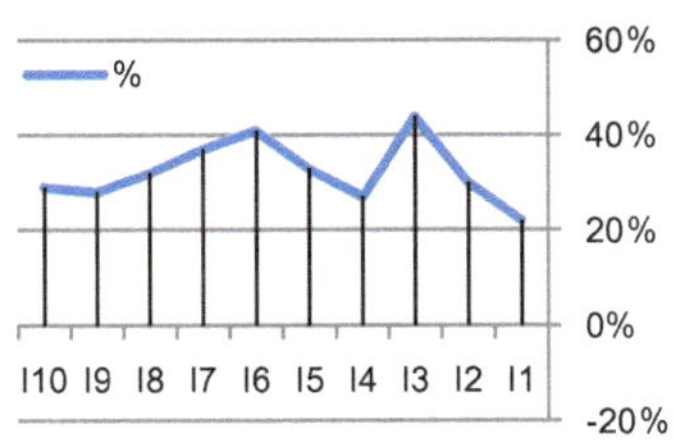

Fig. 3 The linear chart for the first part of the questionnaire (at the end of the study)

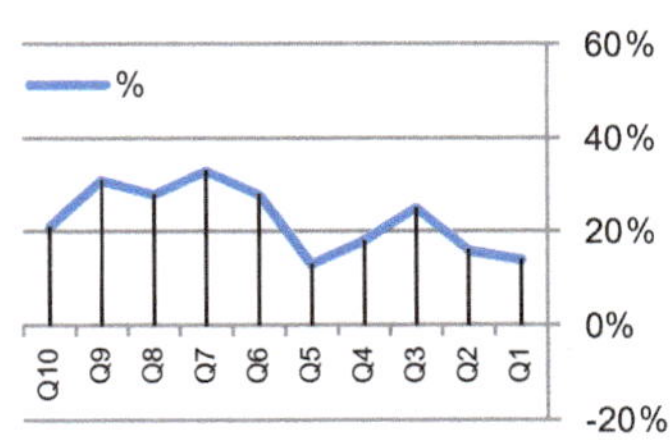

Fig. 4 The linear chart for the second part of the questionnaire (at the end of the study)

8 Conclusion

According to the results we can conclude that

1. There is a strong relationship between using a social network and studying by means of e-learning.
2. The use of a social network will increase the skills of students in e-learning.
3. At the first stage of the questionnaire, we noticed that students used a social network more than at the second stage of the questionnaire.
4. On the other hand, we noticed that students' skills increased gradually through time.
5. The computer skills of students in e-learning increased primarily because of their using the social network.

9 Recommendations

1. The university must encourage students to use the social network by preparing suitable scientific pages or sites.
2. The lecturers have to communicate with their students through a social network by sending and receiving homework and lectures via some type of social media such as Twitter, Facebook, etc.
3. A social network can be a good media to publish lectures or tutorial clips for students; the university or lecturers should build their own channels or sites for this in order to use them in teaching.

References

1. Palová D, Vejacka M (2013) On-line E-learning platform supporting education and practice of accountants in EU space. MIPRO, Opatija, Croatia, pp 641–646
2. Tavangarian D, Leypold ME, Nölting K, Röser M, Voigt D (2004) Is e-Learning the solution for individual learning? Electron J E-Learn 2(2):273–280
3. Laghos A (2007) Assessing the evolution of social networks in e-learning. Unpublished Doctoralthesis, City University London
4. Demiray U (2010) Cases on challenges facing e-learning and national development: institutional studies and practices. e-learning practices, I
5. Guri-Rosenblit S (2005) Distance education and E-Learning: not the same thing. High Educ 49(4):467–493
6. Margolin J, Kleidon B, Williams MPPR (2011) Vermont's title II-D enhancing education through technology program 2010–2011. Final Report. American Institutes for Research, USA -Chicago
7. Al-Shehri AM (2010) E-learning in Saudi Arabia: 'To E or not to E, that is the question'. Med Educ 17(3):147–150

8. Alhojailan M (2012a) The current use and effectiveness of Weblogs as E-Learning tools in higher education. Int Proc Econom Developm Res 27:120–124
9. Alexander S (2001) E-learning developments and experiences. Educ + Train 43(4/5):240–248
10. Solomon G, Schrum L (2007) Web 2.0: new tools, new schools. ISTE (Int Soc Tech Educ)
11. Al-Othman M (2009) Analytical study of the Masters and Ph.D. in education at King Saud in Riyadh during the period 1414 AH to 1427 AH (1993–2009). Masters Dissertation. Saudi Arabia- Riyadh: King Saud University-Educational Department
12. Liccardi I et al (2007) The role of social networks in students' learning experiences. University of Southampton, UK
13. Boyd DM, Ellison NB (2007) Social network sites: definition, history, and scholarship. Michigan State University, USA
14. https://en.wikipedia.org/wiki
15. de Nooy W (2012) Graph theoretical approaches to social network analysis.In: Meyers R (ed) Computational complexity: theory, techniques, and applications. Springer, Heidelberg, pp 2864–2877
16. http://apecsec.org
17. Mohd S, bin Othman A et al (2011) Social network learning: the relationship between characteristics in social network and e-learning websites with learning activities. In: International conference on teaching and learning in higher education (ICTLHE 2011)
18. http://elearningindustry.com

Using IPython for Teaching Web Scraping

Ali Hadi and Malek Al-Zewairi

Abstract Web scraping constitutes an indispensable part of information gathering and data intelligence. IPython has been the *de facto* project for data science since 2001. In this chapter, IPython is employed to support educators in teaching the fundamentals of web scraping. The authors identify providing detailed labs as free online resources together with model answers as the main contribution of this chapter.

Keywords Web scraping · IPython · Education · Learning

1 Introduction

Web scraping is an essential element of the internet era. It is a collection of programming techniques for collecting unstructured information from websites, and then transforming it into structured data [1]. In some literature, web scraping is also referred to as 'web harvesting', in addition to 'web data extraction' [2]. Various disciplines employ web scraping and it has many applications including e-commerce. It represents the core functionality of search engines, i.e., indexing, in which 'web crawlers' (also known as 'bots' and 'web spiders') crawl the Internet, extract data from webpages and index it. Currently, web scraping plays a significant role in web intelligence, web automation, and the semantic web [3].

A. Hadi (✉)
King Hussein Faculty of Computing Sciences, Computer Science Department,
Princess Sumaya University for Technology (PSUT), Amman, Jordan
e-mail: a.hadi@psut.edu.jo

M. Al-Zewairi
The University of Jordan, Amman, Jordan
e-mail: malek.alzewiri@computer.org; malek.alzewiri@jisdf.org

A. Hadi · M. Al-Zewairi
Jordan Information Security and Digital Forensics (JISDF) Research Group, Amman, Jordan

N. Taha et al. (eds.), *Social Media Shaping e-Publishing and Academia*,
DOI 10.1007/978-3-319-55354-2_5

Several programming languages can be natively used for web scraping including Java, Ruby, and Python. Numerous tools, browser plugins, and APIs are available to facilitate web scraping. Table 1.1 compares some of the most popular web scraping tools in terms of software type, license, and programming language.

Table 1.1 List of popular web scraping tools

Web scraper name	Type	License	Programming language	Ref.
Import.io	Standalone software and API	Both free and commercial	RESTful service	[a]
Scrape.it	Plugins	Commercial	N/A	[b]
UiPath	Standalone software and APIs	Commercial	NET framework (APIs)	[c]
ScrapeBox	Standalone software and plugins	Commercial	N/A	[d]
80Legs	Web tool and API	Commercial	RESTful service	[e]
Mozenda	Standalone software	Commercial	N/A	[f]
Kimono	API	Commercial	RESTful service	[g]
OutWit Hub	Standalone software and plugins	Both free and commercial	N/A	[h]
irobotsoft	Standalone software	Free	N/A	[i]
iMacros	Plugins and APIs	Both free and commercial	NET framework (APIs)	[j]
Scrapy	Framework	Open-source	Python 2.7	[k]
awesome-web-scraping	APIs	Open-source	JavaScript, PHP, Ruby, Python	[l]
pjscrape	Framework	Open-source	JavaScript, jQuery	[m]
Grab	Framework	Open-source	Python 2.7, Python 3	[n]

[a]https://www.import.io/
[b]https://scrape.it/
[c]http://www.uipath.com/automate/web-scraping-software
[d]http://www.scrapebox.com/
[e]http://80legs.com/index.html
[f]http://www.mozenda.com/
[g]https://www.kimonolabs.com/
[h]http://www.outwit.com/products/hub/
[i]http://irobotsoft.com/
[j]http://imacros.net/
[k]https://github.com/scrapy/scrapy, http://scrapy.org
[l]https://github.com/lorien/awesome-web-scraping
[m]https://github.com/nrabinowitz/pjscrape, http://nrabinowitz.github.io/pjscrape/
[n]https://github.com/lorien/grab

Web scrapers follow several strategies; a general strategy can be to examine the document object model (DOM) structure of the website, then to examine the source code of the website and finally to determine how the output is to be presented.

The IPython project[1] was first introduced to the scientific community back in 2001 as a free and open-source alternative solution for easy-to-use scientific computing. The project was a result of the amalgamation of two projects: 'LazyPython' and 'Interactive Python Prompt (IPP)'. Initially, IPython was designed to extend Python programming language capabilities by providing[a] web-based interactive environment for data access and visualization, in addition to adding distributed high-performance parallel computing making it highly suitable for scientific programming [4].

In 2011, the project announced a new feature called 'Notebook', which was an instant success. IPython notebook provides an interactive web-based environment to share not only the code but also knowledge conveniently. The new feature allows for the dynamic creation of sharable webpages that comprise rich text, code, plots, LaTeX mathematical equations, multimedia, and widgets in an interactive environment powered by a web server. The project maintains a gallery of prominent IPython notebooks in numerous scientific disciplines shared by the community.[2] With over 20 major scientific fields, the gallery is considered an indispensable teaching instrument for instructors, teachers, and scientists [5].

The client–server architecture of the IPython project and the tremendous success of the IPython notebooks were fundamental factors in the evolution of a new project 'Jupyter'[3] in July 2014. The Jupyter project added support for more than 40 programming languages in addition to the integration of big data. Unlike IPython, the Jupyter project employs a multi-kernels architecture, which allows for support of virtually any number of programming languages. A kernel is an operating system process responsible for executing the code and returning the results, in addition to providing support for several programming features including reflection, type introspection, and tab completion [5].

Chapter "Reaching Your Community via Social Media: Academic Libraries and Librarians Using Facebook and Twitter for Outreach" is intended to be a teaching instrument for educators teaching web scraping, in particular for intermediate users. The authors assume that the reader is familiar with installing IPython and running note books. In case the reader is unfamiliar with IPython, numerous resources are available for learning the basics of IPython [5–7]. A quick and simple guide for installing the latest version of IPython is available online.[4] Five fundamental practices of web scraping will be presented, explained, and discussed in the following section. Moreover, a collection of labs as an online resource are maintained by the authors as online resources for students including model answers for verified instructors.

---

[1]https://github.com/ipython/ipython.

[2]https://github.com/ipython/ipython/wiki/A-gallery-of-interesting-IPython-Notebooks.

[3]http://jupyter.org/.

[4]http://jupyter.readthedocs.org/en/latest/install.html.

2 Five Fundamental Practices for Learning Web Scraping

In this section, six fundamental exercises for learning web scraping will be presented, explained, and discussed using IPython notebook formatting style. The exercises include fetching webpages, URL extraction, working with HTML tags, regular expressions, and performing basic web authentication.

IPython version 4.0 and Python 3.5 are used for all the exercises in this chapter. The steps for setting up a local testing environment and the code for this exercise are both available on the GitHub repository related to this chapter.[5]

2.1 Fetching Webpages

The standard Python library is shipped with `urllib2`,[6] an extensible library for fetching webpages, which is a preliminary activity in web scraping. It is worth noting that in Python 3.x the module `urllib.request` has replaced the old `urllib2.urlopen` module in Python 2.x for URL grapping. The example below fetches a webpage and displays its source code.

```
# Fetch Webpage
import urllib.request
url = 'http://www.jisdf.org/'
webpage = urllib.request.urlopen(url).read()
print(webpage)
```

2.2 URLs Extraction

Extracting all URLs from a website is a fundamental practice in web scraping, which requires parsing each webpage DOM. The `Beautiful Soup` Python library[7] can be extremely helpful in parsing and traversing the DOM tree. The following interactive Python code asks the user to enter the URL for the website and, using the `Beautiful Soup` library, it scrapes the website looking for all URLs.

---

[5]https://github.com/ashemery/pyScraping.

[6]https://docs.python.org/2/library/urllib2.html.

[7]http://www.crummy.com/software/BeautifulSoup/.

```
# Extract URLs
from bs4 import BeautifulSoup
import requests
url = input("Enter the website URL: ")
r  = requests.get("http://" + url)
data = r.text
soup = BeautifulSoup(data)
for link in soup.find_all('a'):
    print(link.get('href'))
```

2.3 *Regular Expressions*

'Regular expressions' is the Swiss army knife for many string operations including searching, matching patterns, and performing find-and-replace. Moreover, regular expressions utilize logical operators (and, or, not), which further enhances its capabilities. Python provides great support for 'regular expressions' under the `re` library[8] in its standard library. In the following code, URL extraction is also performed using regular expressions.

```
import urllib.request
import re
url = 'http://www.psut.edu.jo/'

html = urllib.request.urlopen(url).read()
links = re.findall(b'href="(http://.*?)"', html)
for link in links:
    print (link)
```

2.4 *Working with HTML Tags*

The `Beautiful Soup` library is extremely useful when working with HTML tags. It offers simple yet powerful searching and manipulating of DOM objects. In the code below, the title of the webpage is returned as both DOM object and inner string.

[8]https://docs.python.org/2/library/re.html.

```
# Get Webpage Title
from bs4 import BeautifulSoup
url = 'http://www.jisdf.org'
webpage = urllib.request.urlopen(url).read()
soup = BeautifulSoup(webpage)
soup.title # DOM Object
soup.title.string # String
```

2.5 *Basic Web Authentication*

The ability to handle access control mechanisms is an important part of any web scraping tool. Web or HTTP authentication relies on the WWW-Authenticate response header in addition to the **401**(Access Denied) HTTP status code to provide access control on the web. Several web authentication modes are supported including Basic, Digest, NTLM, and Kerberos. This section will explain how to handle basic web authentication while web scraping.

As the name suggests, basic web authentication is the simplest access control mechanism. The username and password are encoded using Base64 encoding. When trying to access a page protected by basic HTTP authentication, a 401 HTTP status code is returned and the WWW-Authenticate response header is set to 'Basic' as shown in the grayed box below. Additionally, the **realm** string parameter, which defines the pages protected by the same credentials, might be also set in the response. Webpages protected under the same realm share the same credentials, which allows for having multilevel access control within the same domain.

```
HTTP/1.1 401 Access Denied
WWW-Authenticate: Basic realm="Local Server"
```

In the response, the **Authorization** request header is used alongside the basic attribute to pass the value of username and password to the web server by concatenating the value of username and password separated by a colon ':' (e.g., username:password) and encoding the result using Base64 encoding schema. The response below shows the HTTP response packet for the basic web authentication request to the website www.jisdf.org and using username 'admin' and password 'secret'. The Base64 encoded string `YWRtaW46c2VjcmV0` can be decoded using free online tools.[9]

[9]https://www.base64encode.org/.

```
In [16]: import requests.auth
         requests.get('http://www.jisdf.org/private_files/', auth=HTTPBasicAuth('admin', 'secret'))
Out[16]: <Response [200]>
```

Fig. 1 Basic web authenticate request using IPython notebook

Lab 05 Learning HTTP by Doing

Part 04: URL Parsing

The fundamental of how the web is operating, is by using Uniform Resource Locators (URLs). They can point to files on a server, or a resource could be dynamically generated when a request is received. Every URL is comprised of several sections. Python uses the urllib.parse module for working with URLs.

1. From the from urllib.parse module import the urlparse function.

```
In [ ]: # import urlparse function
        from urllib.parse import urlparse
```

2. Use the imported function to parse the following URL "http://www.jisdf.org/about".

```
In [ ]: # Parse URL http://www.jisdf.org/about
        url = urlparse('http://www.jisdf.org/about')
```

3. Print the received results. Is it cleary how the URLs are being parsed?

```
In [ ]: # Print the results
        print(url)
```

Another useful function that the urllib.parse module provides is the urljoin function. This function could be used to create a full URL.

4. Using the urljoin function, modify your code to print full URL.

```
In [ ]: # Print full URL
        absoluteUrl = urljoin(url[0] + '://' + url[1], url[2])
        print(absoluteUrl)
```

Fig. 2 Excerpt of lab 05 showing model answer

```
GET /private_files/ HTTP/1.1
Host: www.jisdf.org
Authorization: Basic YWRtaW46c2VjcmV0
```

In Python, the `requests` library[10] can be used to perform basic web authentication. The code for sending/receiving abasic HTTP authentication request/response using IPython is shown in Fig. 1. The `httpbin` service can be used to prepare a local testing environment.

[10]https://pypi.python.org/pypi/requests.

3 Web Scraping Labs

A collection of ten labs is maintained as online resources for students and the model answers are included for verified instructors. An excerpt from the fifth lab is shown in Fig. 2 with the model answer using IPython notebook style. The lab explains URL parsing by example. The student is asked to perform several URL parsing and manipulation tasks using IPython.

References

1. Le QT, Pishva D (2015) Application of web scraping and Google API service to optimize convenience stores' distribution. In: 17th International conference on advanced communication technology (ICACT). pp 478–482
2. Vargiu E, Urru M (2012) Exploiting web scraping in a collaborative filtering-based approach to web advertising. Artif Intell Res 2:44–54. doi:10.5430/air.v2n1p44
3. Malik SK, Rizvi S (2011) Information extraction using web usage mining, web scraping and semantic annotation. In: Proceedings of the 2011 international conference on computational intelligence and communication networks. IEEE Computer Society, Washington, DC, USA, pp 465–469
4. Pérez F, Granger BE (2007) IPython: a system for interactive scientific computing. Comput Sci Eng 9:21–29. doi:10.1109/MCSE.2007.53
5. Rossant C (2014) IPython interactive computing and visualization cookbook. Packt Publishing
6. Martins LF (2014) IPython notebook essentials. Packt Publishing
7. Rossant C (2015) Learning IPython for interactive computing and data visualization 2nd edn. Packt Publishing

The Role of Social Network Sites in Connecting Students with Learning and Academic Activities: A Case Study

Dina Tbaishat

Abstract Social Network Sites (SNSs) are becoming increasingly popular as means of communication. Much research has been carried out to investigate the use of SNSs in various contexts, such as education. Students are becoming more interested in incorporating social network sites into their academic lives to support learning. It is important to understand how students use SNSs outside the conventional classroom context, as this could provide an insight into how to apply SNSs formally for academic purposes. This study is carried out to investigate the use of SNSs among undergraduate students in an attempt to support their learning and academic activities. Social network sites offer plenty of opportunities to communicate and interact. They can also be used to support learning and academic activities in general. The research strategy used is descriptive survey research design; data was collected using questionnaires. The sample size is 63 students from the library and information science department at the University of Jordan. The results revealed that all students use at least one social network site. The results also showed how students connect for the purpose of learning or for any other academic activity. Recommendations are drawn from the findings regarding the use of social network sites among students and the role that academics may play to further encourage the phenomenon.

Keywords Social network sites · Social communication · Undergraduate students · Facebook

1 Introduction

Social Network Sites (SNSs) have become a phenomenon that has gained popularity over the last decade; they became an innovative way for individuals and organizations to communicate, where people use various social network sites to

D. Tbaishat (✉)
University of Jordan, Amman, Jordan
e-mail: d.tbishat@ju.edu.jo

N. Taha et al. (eds.), *Social Media Shaping e-Publishing and Academia*,
DOI 10.1007/978-3-319-55354-2_6

communicate personally and professionally. SNSs are also attracting students' attention in particular; for instance, Sponcil and Gitimu [23] found that all college students—under study—were using some form of social networking websites. This growing audience has increased the potential of SNSs to establish relationships and maintain connections among students. For educational and academic activities purposes, SNSs have changed the way students interact. The purpose of this study is to explore to what extent selected undergraduate students at the University of Jordan actually use SNSs. The study also examines the role of SNSs in supporting learning and academic activities, taking into consideration any challenges they might face when using SNSs for academic purposes.

2 Learning and Academic Activities

Learning is a broad concept that includes multiple acts such as: acquiring knowledge, skills, values and good behavior. This research investigates how SNSs can be used by a particular group of students as an educational tool to learn about the subject area and to develop various skills. The research also investigates how SNSs can be used to connect students with academic activities. Academic activities within universities mainly include teaching and research—at various levels. The concept of academic activities is usually derived from the academic institution's vision and requirements. According to the University of Canterbury [25], "academic activities arise from requirements to meet the University's obligations and from the initiatives of individual staff members." The University considers five elements comprising academic activities; these are: teaching, research, departmental services, university services, and professional services. Different universities embrace a range of academic activities, but consider teaching and research on the top of the list. The EU Business School [10] has a broader definition for academic activities to include all related seminars outside the classroom; it states that academic activities "give students an insight into the world outside the classroom. These seminars, presentations and trips complement the theory that students learn in class, offering hands-on experiences that bring the business world to life". [2] looked at perspectives of academic activities in seven universities in Pakistan. The authors assessed academic activities through the following elements: teaching, research, staff development, leadership development opportunities for students, assessment, curriculum, and cooperative learning.

For this research, the main elements investigated within learning are:

1. Can SNSs be used as educational tools for learning purposes?
2. Can SNSs help improve students' English language skills?
3. Can SNSs help improve students' communication skills?
4. Are SNSs efficient educational tools compared to conventional teaching methods?

5. Can SNSs be used to provide academic feedback to students?
6. Can SNSs be used to share material between students?
7. Can SNSs be used to discuss assignments?
8. Can SNSs be used for self learning?

While the main elements investigated within academic activities are:

1. Can SNSs be used to promote/make announcements about academic activities (such as conferences, workshops and exhibitions)?
2. Are SNSs exploited to promote library services?
3. Is there real communication between students and university staff via SNSs regarding any academic activity?
4. What are the best SNS that can be used to support academic activities?

3 Literature Review

Social Network Sites have been increasingly used by individuals and within organizations for various purposes: some organizations use them as tools for communication within employees [15]; others consider them useful tools for innovation, enhancing customer service, developing stakeholder collaboration, and enhancing marketing activities [22]. In addition, SNSs proved to be useful tools within the academic library environment, as stated by Hamad et al. [12], where SNSs can be used for the purpose of enhancing librarians' professional skills.

When it comes to the learning environment, some of the previous literature showed that there has not yet been much research investigating the educational use of social network sites [9]. Instead, the trend was toward students' usage habits of social networks and the most popular SNS rather than how these can be integrated into the learning environment. For instance, Davis et al. [6] state that there is limited research on the use of social media technology among college students, and that the assessment of the impact of social media technology on students' achievement and attitude is rare. Bicen and Cavus [3] found that Facebook and Hi5 were the most preferred social network sites used by undergraduate students at the department of computer education at the Near East University in Cyprus. The authors, however, stated that research should be conducted on how such tools may be used in education. Doğruer et al. [7] examined the motivation factors of using Facebook by the English Preparatory School of Eastern Mediterranean University students. Five items were investigated in this study as motivations, and the results showed that 39% of students use Facebook to pass the time, 60% of students use it to communicate better, and almost half of the students use Facebook for entertainment. Bijari et al. [5] found that communication with old friends was the most common reason for using social networks by students, and that there is no relation between using SNSs and students' GPA. Bicen and Cavus [4] looked at undergraduate students' usage habits for Facebook; they found that students use Facebook intensively to communicate, and to share photos, news, and links.

On the other hand, recent research transcended this stage and began to investigate SNSs in relation to learning. SNSs can be implemented in the academic environment to support learning and academic activities. Research has started to investigate this topic and support integrating social networks sites into the learning environment. Wolfe [27] stressed the need for the classroom experience to keep pace with the growing interactivity through online tools and SNSs, considering such tools a great way of changing students' attitudes toward learning, from one way communication to a more interactive group-oriented environment. Eren [9] investigated students' attitudes toward the use of Facebook in language classrooms. It was found that students' attitudes toward this activity are very positive; the interview results showed that students support the idea of integrating social network sites into their traditional classroom. In another research study by [26], it was found that students used their personal SNSs to discuss academic-related topics, such as sharing experience about undertaking some work. It was also noted that the frequency of SNS use for such purposes greatly increased at some points, particularly when assignments deadlines are close or at the examinations period; this suggests that SNSs play a crucial role in students' academic experiences. In a similar study, [8] found that social networking is popular amongst students at the University of Nigeria Nsukka. The results found that students use social networking to interact with each other, and connect with their classmates for online study. Moreover, Thaiposri and Wannapiroon [24] found that students could enhance their critical thinking skills and communicate better through use of social networks.

SNSs are also utilized by community colleges to connect and deliver information to students. Davis et al. [6] produced a survey report about the role of social media in community colleges within 378 community colleges randomly selected in the United States. The leaders of those community colleges think that social media can play an integral role in many aspects such as information distribution, marketing, enhancing communication, enhancing instruction and classroom discussion. Some universities have already integrated SNSs as means of communication; according to Mallia [17], Southampton Solent University in the UK has official Facebook and Twitter communication channels which have a huge number of 'likes'. They are best used for making announcements and connecting to students about various events. On the other hand, according to Davis et al. [6], admissions offices at some universities have started using students' blogs to showcase current student experiences as a recruitment tool for prospective students.

Some studies are encouraging moving from learning management systems to social network sites. For instance; [19] found that it is important to follow an integrated approach to the application of learning management systems and social networks in the process of learning. The results are based on a survey of students and teachers at the National Research Tomsk State University, Russia. Madleňák et al. [16] suggested two main variants of realization of social networks for the electronic support of education at the University of Žilina – Slovakia, since students were dissatisfied with the existing state of information provided via the university Moodle. The first variant supports using Facebook combined with e-learning together with the current Moodle. The second one suggests creating a special social network site specifically for the needs of Žilina University. Another research study that supports the idea of moving from learning management systems to social networks is the work undertaken by Garavaglia and Petti [11] where the authors believe that it is crucial that universities observe students' habits to be ready for the next change (in this case students tend to use mobile devices and social networks to resolve needs; hence, universities should act accordingly).

4 Research Problem

According to Eren [9], little research to date has investigated the educational use of social network sites. Davis et al. [6] state that there is limited research on the use of social media technology among college students, and that the assessment of the impact of social media technology on students' achievement and attitude is rare. However, recent research has attempted to fill this gap by investigating SNSs in relation to learning (as demonstrated in Sect. 2). Therefore, considering the great potential of SNSs for educational purposes, and the great interest among students in SNSs, this research was conducted to explore to what extent selected undergraduate students at the University of Jordan use SNSs for academic purposes, and to examine potential challenges students might face when using them.

5 Research Objectives

This study is conducted to:

1. Examine the extent of usage of SNSs among undergraduate students at the University of Jordan—within the library and information science department in particular.
2. Explore the role of SNSs in connecting students with learning and academic activities.
3. Make recommendations regarding integrating SNSs further within the educational system at the organization under study, including highlighting the role that academics might play to further encourage the phenomenon.

6 Methodology and Data Collection Method

6.1 The Sample

The study adopted the descriptive survey research design which was employed to derive responses from a sample size of 63 undergraduate students. The sample only represented undergraduate students from the library and information science department at the University of Jordan. The total number of students in the department is 126—only students from the second year and upward were considered. The researcher involvement in this department is the justification behind choosing this sample group. Data was collected from respondents using questionnaires. The 63 respondents all completed and returned the questionnaire correctly, representing a 100% response rate as shown in Table 1. The University of Jordan is one of the largest public universities in Jordan that comprises 18 faculties. The sample is selected from library and information science students in the Faculty of Educational Sciences. Therefore, it is worth mentioning that the selected sample does not represent the University of Jordan, rather; it provides an insight into the necessity of integrating social network sites into the learning environment, in parallel with the existing literature.

6.2 The Questionnaire

To investigate the role of SNSs in connecting students with educational and academic activities, a questionnaire was prepared and distributed to 63 undergraduate students from the library and information science department at the University of Jordan. The first part of the questionnaire gathered demographic information, which was considered later as possible factors that might affect the results (see Sect. 8). The second part of the questionnaire consisted of five items, in an attempt to learn about students' usage of SNSs, and the purpose for using them. The third part of the questionnaire consisted of 18 items to clarify SNSs' role in supporting education

Table 1 Response rates information

	Total no. of students in the department	No. of students (sample selected)	Responses	Percentage of sample selected to total students' number (%)	Percentage of individual student's responses (%)
University of Jordan – library and information science department	126	63	63	50	100

Table 2 The weights used to determine the degree of agreement for each item

Degree	Mean
Weak	3.68–5
Moderate	2.34–3.67
High	1–2.33

and specific academic activities; it also highlighted favorite SNSs suitable for these purposes. The last part of the questionnaire looked at some possible challenges that students might face when using SNSs for academic purposes; these were expressed through five items. A copy of the questionnaire can be found in appendix 1.

A Likert scale was applied to weigh the degree of agreement with the questionnaire items. Table 2 next demonstrates the range of weights used to determine the degree of agreement for each item using the mean value, where 'high' means agreement.

7 Statistical Analysis—The Results

Mean and standard deviation were calculated to assess the degree of agreement with items in order to discover students' perceptions of SNSs' role in connecting students with educational and academic activities. One way ANOVA analysis was conducted to investigate the existence of any statistical differences, at significance level ($\alpha \leq 0.05$) using f-test, between responses based on different variables. The next four Sects. (7.1–7.4) demonstrate the results of the statistical analysis.

7.1 Demographic Information

Part one in the questionnaire gathered demographic information and identified three factors expected to affect the results. Table 3 next demonstrates the distribution of the study sample based on these factors that might affect the respondents' perception and attitude towards the use of social network sites in the learning environment. The varying factors are: current year of study, gender, and age.

7.2 The Extent of Usage of SNSs Among Undergraduate Students

Part two of the questionnaire considered items related to the extent of usage of SNSs among undergraduate students. This part included five questions. The results indicated that all students actually use SNSs. Respondents indicated that they are

Table 3 Total study sample distribution based on variant factors

% of the sample (rounded)	No. of students from the sample	Variable type	Factor/Variable (%)
Current year of study	Second year	12	19
	Third year	27	42.9
	Fourth year	22	34.9
	Other	2	3.2
Gender	Male	5	7.9
	Female	58	92
Age	Less than 20	6	9.5
	20–25	57	90.5
	26–30	0	0
	>30	0	0

Table 4 The number of students using each SNS

Which SNS do you use?	Number of students	Percentage (rounded) (%)
Facebook	56	88.8
Twitter	15	23.8
Google+	26	41.3
LinkedIn	4	6.3
Other	20	31.7

Table 5 The number of students using SNS for specific purpose

What are your purposes of using SNSs?	Number of students	Percentage (rounded) (%)
Keep in touch	46	73
Find general information	39	61.9
Find study-related information	40	63.5
Meet new people	28	44.4
Other	4	6.3

frequent users of SNSs—most students use SNSs on a daily basis. The variable 'time spent on SNSs' indicated that students spend on average 5 to 6 h a day on SNSs.

The results also provided insight into which SNSs students use the most and for what purposes. Tables 4 and 5 below show the number of users for each SNS (Table 4) and the purpose for using the site (Table 5).

As can be seen in Table 4, Facebook wins ground when it comes to popularity. Students seem to prefer Facebook over other SNSs in general, as 88.8% of students use Facebook. The second SNS most frequently used is Google+ (41.3%). It was noted that some students use other SNSs besides the choices given to them in the questionnaire such as: WhatsApp and Instagram. However, WhatsApp is not considered a social network site; instead, it is more like an instant messaging application.

As noted in Table 5, students use SNSs mostly to 'keep in touch' with others and to stay connected. The second purpose for using SNSs is to 'find study-related information', which is of interest for this research whose main aim is to discover whether SNSs are utilized by students for academic purposes.

7.3 The Role of SNSs in Supporting Education and Academic Activities—Discussion

Part three of the questionnaire investigated the role of SNSs in supporting educational and academic activities through 18 questions, providing the following results:

1. Students believe that SNSs can be used as educational tools, and also to promote academic activities, with mean values of 1.75 and 1.60, and standard deviation of 0.761 and 0.636, respectively.
2. Students believe that SNSs help improve their English language and communication skills, with mean values of 1.98 and 1.86, and standard deviation of 0.833 and 0.715, respectively. This is an important point for students from the library and information science department as their English language skills need to be improved since most library and information science courses are taught in English. Research in the literature supports this statement; for instance, Alfaki and Alharthy [1] examined the possibility of using SNSs to promote English language learning amongst 70 students at college level. It was found that SNSs can actually enhance language learning. The results showed that SNSs offer a chance for learners to overcome the tension of classrooms; they also provide collaboration and interactivity, which help learn the language better. For improving communication skills, the results of this work agree with the findings of the literature as set out in Sect. 3: [5, 6, 15, 17].
3. When students were asked whether SNSs are efficient educational tools compared to traditional ones, the results provided a mean of 2.48 and a standard deviation of 0.965; the response results represent moderate agreement. Further, 48% of students think that SNSs are efficient educational tools compared to traditional ones, while 29% are neutral about the statement, and only 13% disagree.
4. Most students wish that their tutors incorporate SNSs more into the learning and teaching process; they also think that the university library should exploit SNSs more to promote its services. The mean values are 1.94 and 1.70, with standard deviation of 0.896 and 0.816, respectively. The results reflect students'

awareness of the value of SNSs in relation to learning, and also indicate their desire to better connect with their university library though SNSs. This can be implemented by creating groups on Facebook or similar social network sites to involve students in the library's activities and to enable librarians to promote their library services.

5. The final results in this part of the questionnaire showed that students do use SNSs for academic purposes; for instance, 92% of students stated that they use SNSs to discuss assignments, 87% of students share materials related to their study such as PowerPoint slides and related articles, and 84% of students use SNSs for self-learning. Regarding tutors, 84% of students revealed that some of their tutors use SNSs for educational purposes and 65% of students stated that some of their tutors use SNSs to support academic activities.

The detailed results regarding which SNSs are more suitable as educational tools and for making announcements about academic activities follow in Table 6.

The results in Table 6 show that most students (81%) believe that Facebook is an appropriate and suitable SNS to be utilized within the university as an educational tool and also to support any academic activity. The actual use of Facebook for these purposes supports the previous statement; 63% of students actually use Facebook as an educational tool and to learn about academic activities. Google+ comes next with 32% of students using it for educational purposes; however, it is less preferred when it comes to supporting academic activities (only 12.7% of students agree with the statement). Many studies in the literature show that Facebook is the most common communication tool among university students: for instance, Bicen and Cavus [4] looked at undergraduate students' usage habits of Facebook; they concluded that future studies should concentrate on integrating Facebook into education and teaching since students spend significant amounts of time using Facebook. In later studies, Işık [14] found that most of the north school teachers in Cyprus use Facebook to post assignments and to share selected YouTube videos to visualize their lessons. They also use it to exchange information and answer students' questions, especially during the examinations period. [21] found that Facebook has high impact on learning performance; consequently, it should receive growing attention from practitioners and information systems researchers. On the other hand, it is worth mentioning that Facebook is not the only SNS suitable for learning; for instance, [18] consider Twitter a good tool to be used in university research, teaching and impact activities; it can be used to create an account for each course, and use tweets to advise on tasks. Moreover, it can be used in research projects when announcing new publications using hash tags for more visible material.

In the same section of the questionnaire, students were asked whether they receive any feedback from tutors via SNSs, whether they discuss assignments or share material with other students, and if they use SNSs for self-learning. The

Table 6 Four questions in part three of the questionnaire specifying which SNSs are used or considered most suitable as educational tools and for academic activities, from the students' perspective

SNS students think is most suitable as an educational tool	Number of students	Percentage (rounded) (%)
Facebook	51	81
Twitter	1	1.6
Google+	20	31.7
LinkedIn	1	1.6
Other	4	6.3
None	3	4.8
SNS students think is most suitable to support academic activities	Number of students	Percentage (rounded) (%)
Facebook	51	63
Twitter	13	20.6
Google+	8	12.7
LinkedIn	2	3.2
Other	2	3.2
None	3	4.8
SNS students actually use as an educational tool	Number of students	Percentage (rounded) (%)
Facebook	40	63.5
Twitter	1	1.6
Google+	20	31.7
LinkedIn	0	0
Other	2	3.2
None	12	19
SNS students actually use to keep up with academic activities	Number of students	Percentage (rounded) (%)
Facebook	51	63
Twitter	2	3.2
Google+	8	12.7
LinkedIn	0	0
Other	2	3.2
None	2	3.2

results showed high usage of SNSs for these purposes, with means of 1.54, 1.11, 1.13, and 1.16 respectively.

Table 7 Suggested reasons for not using SNSs for educational purposes

Reason for not using SNSs for educational purposes	Mean	Standard deviation
Not having internet connection at home	4.21	1.124
Not having a smart phone	4.35	1.003
SNSs are not used by our tutors for educational purposes	4.06	1.061
SNSs can only cover few aspects in education	3.40	1.225

7.4 The Challenges Students Might Face When Using SNSs for Academic Purposes

Many of students believe that there are challenges associated with the use of SNSs for educational purposes, with a mean of 2.25 and standard deviation of 0.842. However, none of the challenges listed in the questionnaire were actually faced by students; most students disagreed with the statements, as shown in Table 7.

Note that the last reason (SNSs covering only few aspects of education) got the lowest mean value (3.40) which indicates that some students actually believe that it is a reason why SNSs are not fully utilized for educational purposes. There must be other strong challenges when using SNSs to support education; this can be a topic for future research, as discussed in Sect. 10.

8 Effect of Possible Factors on Results

It is crucial to investigate whether any of the factors (mentioned previously in Table 3) affect responses. There are three factors considered: current year of study, gender and age. F-test analysis was conducted for each variable to assess its effect, considering the factor significant if the significance level is less than 0.05.

For the first factor 'current year of study' it was noted that it is not a significant factor as the significance levels for all statements were not less than (0.05), except for one statement. When students were asked about using SNSs to support academic activities, the significance level was 0.017 which is less than 0.05; this means that the mean values of responses to this question varied between respondents with different years of study.

The same applies for the second factor 'gender', where it did not affect any responses except for the question related to using SNSs to support academic activities, with a significance level of 0.028. This indicates that the mean values of responses to this question varied between respondents according to gender.

The last factor 'age', did not affect any of the statements, with no significance level less than 0.05. The analysis suggested that there were no statistically significant differences at significance level ≤ 0.05 between the means of responses.

9 Recommendations

1. According to students' responses to the statement "I wish that my tutors incorporate SNSs more into their teaching strategies," with a mean value of 1.94, it is recommended that SNSs get more attention by academics to be integrated within the learning environment. Tutors can enhance the learning process by introducing social media into the classroom. Evidence from the literature shows that there have been attempts to leverage SNSs such as Facebook for the benefit of learning and teaching. Many innovative practices can be used in this context such as: sharing material through Facebook; setting up class blogs and Facebook groups; using Twitter for instructional support; using Wikis for lesson summaries [17]; sharing material and learning outcomes through Facebook.
2. It is also important to integrate SNSs into the library environment, as the mean value for this statement scored 1.70. The library can announce new events and services through social network sites rather than through conventional methods, consequently attracting many students. Librarians can also use SNSs to share interests and experience [20].
3. To achieve this, raising awareness about the value of SNSs in the academic environment is crucial. The university can adopt marketing strategies for this purpose; it could start by creating a Facebook group.

10 Limitations and Future Work

As mentioned previously in Sect. 6.1, the researcher selected a sample from library and information science undergraduate students at the University of Jordan. Therefore, the sample does not represent the University of Jordan. Results in this research cannot be generalized; however, they can act as an insight into how SNSs can be exploited to serve academic needs at the University of Jordan. Further research—on a wider base—can build on this.

Moreover, as many students believe that there are a number of challenges associated with the use of SNSs for educational purposes, with a mean of 2.25 and standard deviation of 0.842, and as none of the suggested challenges in the questionnaire were actually faced by students, then it is worth investigating what kind of challenges students may face when using SNSs.

11 Conclusion

Social network sites have been attracting students' attention as they are considered a robust communication channel. 90% of college students have profiles on Facebook [13]. This study was conducted to investigate the role of SNSs in connecting library science students at the University of Jordan to academic activities. Descriptive survey research design was employed to derive responses from a sample size of 63 undergraduate students. The data collection method used was a questionnaire, and the response rate was 100%. The results revealed full usage of SNSs among students for different purposes, where Facebook is the most popular communication tool. The results also highlighted that 63.5% of students use SNSs to find study-related information, discuss assignments and share material. Most importantly; the results show that most students wish that their tutors incorporate SNSs more into the learning and teaching process; they also think that the university library should exploit SNSs more to promote its services.

Finally, none of the external factors (current year of study, gender, age) affected the results significantly, except for one statement (SNSs can be used to support academic activities), where it was found that both 'current year of study' and 'gender' affect the responses significantly.

Appendix 1: The Questionnaire

The role of social network sites in connecting students with learning and academic activities: a case study

Kindly find a few minutes to fill in this questionnaire, which is intended to investigate the use of Social Networks Sites (SNSs) among undergraduate students of the library and information science department at the University of Jordan, in an attempt to support their learning and academic activities. The data gathered through this questionnaire is totally anonymous and will only be used for the purpose of this research. The questionnaire consists of four parts as follows:

Part one: Demographic information. Please tick the boxes as appropriate:					
Year of study:	☐ first year	☐ second year	☐ third year	☐ fourth year	☐ other
Gender:	☐ male	☐ female			
Age:	☐ less than 20	☐ 20–25	☐ 26–30	☐ >30	

Part two: The extent of usage of Social Network Sites (SNSs) among undergraduate students. Please tick your choice.

Q. num	Question					
1	Do you use social network sites (SNSs)?	Yes ☐	No ☐			
2	If yes, which of these do you use?	Facebook ☐	Twitter ☐	Google+ ☐	Linkedin ☐	Other (specify) ☐
3	How frequently do you visit SNSs?	Daily ☐	More than once a week ☐	Weekly ☐	Monthly ☐	Don't use it ☐
4	How much time do you spend on SNSs in a day?	< 2 hours ☐	2-4 hours ☐	5-6 hours ☐	> 6 hours ☐	don't use it ☐
5	What are your purposes for using SNSs?	Keep in touch ☐	Find general info. ☐	Find study related info. ☐	Meet new people ☐	Other (specify) ☐

Part three: The role of SNSs in supporting education/academic activities. Please write X where appropriate.

Item num	Items	Strongly agree	Agree	Neutral	Disagree	Strongly disagree
6	SNSs can be used as educational tools					
7	SNSs can be used to promote / make announcements about academic activities (such as conferences, workshops and exhibitions)					
8	SNSs help improve your English language					
9	SNSs help improve your communication skills					
10	SNSs are efficient as educational tools compared to conventional teaching					
11	I wish that my tutors incorporate SNSs more into their teaching strategies					
12	Our university library should exploit SNSs to promote its services					

Q. num	Question						
13	Which SNS do you think is the most suitable as an educational tool?	Facebook ☐	Twitter ☐	Google+ ☐	Linkedin ☐	Other (specify) ☐	None ☐
14	Which SNS do you think is the most suitable to support academic activities?	Facebook ☐	Twitter ☐	Google+ ☐	Linkedin ☐	Other (specify) ☐	None ☐
15	Which SNS do you actually use as an educational tool?	Facebook ☐	Twitter ☐	Google+ ☐	Linkedin ☐	Other (specify) ☐	None ☐
16	Which SNS do you actually use to keep up with academic activities?	Facebook ☐	Twitter ☐	Google+ ☐	Linkedin ☐	Other (specify) ☐	None ☐
17	Do you have any contact with any tutor via SNSs?	Yes ☐	No ☐				
18	Are there any tutors – of those who teach you – who actually use SNSs for educational purposes? If yes please specify	Yes ☐	No ☐				
19	Are there any tutors – of those who teach you – who actually use SNSs for academic activities? If yes please specify	Yes ☐	No ☐				
20	Do you get any academic feedback from your tutors through SNSs?	Yes ☐	No ☐				
21	Do you discuss assignments with other students via SNSs?	Yes ☐	No ☐				
22	Do you share material documents (such as Power-Point slides) with other students via SNSs?	Yes ☐	No ☐				
23	Do you use SNSs for self-learning?	Yes ☐	No ☐				

Part four: The challenges students face when using SNSs for educational purposes and academic activities.

Item num	Items	Strongly agree	Agree	Neutral	Disagree	Strongly disagree
24	There are some challenges related to using SNSs to support learning and academic activities					
25	I don't use SNSs for educational purposes and academic activities because I don't have internet connection at home					
26	I don't use SNSs for educational purposes and academic activities because I don't have a smart phone that makes it much easier to connect					
27	I don't use SNSs for educational purposes and academic activities because SNSs are not used by our tutors for educational purposes					
28	I don't use SNSs for educational purposes and academic activities because I think they can only cover a few aspects in education					

Any other comments? --

Thank you for finding the time to complete this questionnaire
Dr. Dina Tbaishat

Appendix 2: Statistical Analysis (Results)

Descriptive Statistics

	N	Minimum	Maximum	Mean	Std. Deviation
Time spent on SNS	63	1	4	2.25	1.062
Use of SNS	63	1	1	1.00	.000
How frequently used	63	1	3	1.33	.648
SNS can be used to support education	63	1	5	1.75	.761
SNS can be used to support academic activities	63	1	3	1.60	.636
SNS can be used to improve English	63	1	4	1.98	.833
SNS can be used to improve communication skills	63	1	3	1.86	.715
SNS are good tools compared to conventional ones	63	1	5	2.48	.965
I wish tutors used SNS	63	1	5	1.94	.896
I wish our library used SNS	63	1	5	1.70	.816
Do you have contact with tutors via SNS	63	1	2	1.22	.419
Does any tutor actually use SNS for education	63	1	2	1.16	.368
Does any tutor actually use SNS for academic activities	63	1	2	1.35	.481
Do you get feedback from your tutor via SNS	63	1	2	1.54	.502
Do you discuss assignments with students via SNS	63	1	2	1.11	.317
Do you share material with students via SNS	63	1	2	1.13	.336
Do you use SNS for self-learning	63	1	2	1.16	.368
There are challenges	63	1	4	2.25	.842
I don't use SNS because I don't have internet access	63	1	5	4.21	1.124
I don't use SNS because I don't have a smart phone	63	1	5	4.35	1.003
I don't use SNS because tutors don't use it	63	1	5	4.06	1.061
I don't use SNS because they cover only few aspects	63	1	5	3.40	1.225
Valid N (listwise)	63				

References

1. Alfaki I, Alharthy K (2014) Towards a digital world: using social networks to promote learner's language. Am Int J Contemp Res 4(10):105–114
2. Ali A, Tariq RH, Topping J (2013) Perspectives of academic activities in universities in Pakistan. J Further High Educ 37(3):321–348
3. Bicen H, Cavus N (2010) The most preferred social network sites by students. Procedia Soc Behav Sci 2(2):5864–5869
4. Bicen H, Cavus N (2011) Social network sites usage habits of undergraduate students: a case study of Facebook. Procedia Soc Behav Sci 28:943–947
5. Bijari B, Alireza J, Erfanian M, Abedini MR, Abassi A (2013) The impact of virtual social networks on students' academic achievement in Birjand University of Medical Sciences in East Iran. Procedia Soc Behav Sci 83:103–106
6. Davis III C H F, Deil−Amen R, Rios−Aguilar C, and González Canché, MS (2012) Social media and higher education: A literature review and research directions. Report printed by the University of Arizona and Claremont Graduate University.
7. Doğruer et al (2011) What is the motivation for using Facebook? Procedia Soc Behav Sci 15:2642–2646
8. Eke H, Omekwu C, Odoh J (2014) The use of social networking sites among the undergraduate students of University of Nigeria, Nsukka. Library Philosophy and Practice (e-journal). p. 1195. Retrieved from http://digitalcommons.unl.edu/libphilprac/1195
9. Eren O (2012) Students' attitudes towards using social networking in foreign languages classes: a Facebook example. Int J Bus Soc Sci 3(20):288–294
10. EU Business School (2015) EU Business school academic activities. Retrieved from https://www.euruni.edu/euruni/Academic/Academic-Activities/EU-Business-School-Academic-Activities.html
11. Garavaglia A, Petti L (2015) University student communities and media habits: from formal LMS to social networks. Procedia Soc Behav Sci 197:898–903
12. Hamad F, Tbaishat D and Fadel M (2015) Value of social networks in academic libraries: a case study. Paper presented at the sixth international conference on education in a new digital environment, 7–6 May, Zarqa, Jordan
13. Harvard Institute on Politics (2011) IOP youth polling: Spring 2011 survey. Harvard University, Kennedy School of Government, Cambridge
14. Işık F (2013) Comparison of the use of social network in education between North and South Cyprus. Procedia Soc Behav Sci 103:210–219
15. Leonardi PM, Huysman M, Steinfield C (2013) Enterprise social media: Definition, history, and prospects for the study of social technologies in organizations. J Comput Mediated Commun 19:1–19
16. Madleňák R, Madleňáková L, Kianičková E (2015) Designing a social network to support e-learning activities at the Department of Communications, University of Žilina. Procedia Soc Behav Sci 176:103–110
17. Mallia G (2013) The Social Classroom: Integrating Social Network Use in Education. Information Science Reference, USA
18. Mollett A, Moran D, Dunleavy P (2011) Using Twitter in university research, teaching and impact activities. Impact of social sciences: maximizing the impact of academic research, LSE Public Policy Group, London School of Economics and Political Science., London, UK. Retrieved from http://eprints.lse.ac.uk/38489/
19. Mozhaeva G, Feshchenko A, Kulikov I (2014) E-learning in the evaluation of students and teachers: LMS or social networks? Procedia Soc Behav Sci 152:127–130
20. Parveen N (2011) Use of social networking site (Facebook) in making awareness among the library and information science professionals of university libraries of U.P: a case study. Int J Digital Libr Serv 1:9–17

21. Sánchez-Franco MJ, Villarejo-Ramos ÁF, Martín-Velicia FA (2011) Social integration and post-adoption usage of social network sites an analysis of effects on learning performance. Procedia Soc Behav Sci 15:256–262
22. Singh M, Peszynski K (2014) Organisational value of social technologies: an Australian study. Electron J Inf Syst Evaluation 17(1):088–099
23. Sponcil MNS, Gitimu P (2013) Use of social media by college students: relationship to communication and self-concept. J Technol Res 4:1–13
24. Thaiposr P, Wannapiroon P (2015) Enhancing students' critical thinking skills through teaching and learning by inquiry-based learning activities using social network and cloud computing. Procedia Soc Behav Sci 174:2137–2144
25. University of Canterbury (2015) Allocation of academic activities and establishing academic staff workload policy. v.1.03. Retrieved from www.canterbury.ac.nz
26. Vivian R, Barnes A, Geer R, Wood D (2014) The academic journey of university students on Facebook: an analysis of informal academic-related activity over a semester. Res Learn Technol, **22**
27. Wolfe AM (2007) Student attitudes towards social networks and learning modalities. In: Midwest business administration association (MBAA) International Spring Conference, Chicago, Illinois

An Investigation of Social Media and E-Publishing Usage Among Jordanian University Students

Riyad F. Hussein

Abstract The study reported in this chapter investigated social networking sites (SNS) and e-publishing usage among undergraduate students at the University of Jordan. For this purpose, a 25-item questionnaire was developed, piloted and then administered to a sample of 240 respondents in the faculties of foreign languages and information technology. The questionnaire investigated three major issues: the extent of SNS usage such as Facebook and Twitter; e-publishing usage such as blogs, e-books, e-journals, online newspapers, and digital library; and finally the dangers or fears associated with SNS usage. Results indicated a widespread usage of SNS and a strong attachment to the SNS in general such as Facebook and to less popular ones such as Twitter, Instagram, and Snapchat, generally used to connect people from near and far. The respondents emphasized SNS as a means of socialization more than a learning medium, so sharing and exchanging information was the norm and e-publishing such as blogs, e-books, e-journals, online newspapers, and digital library usage was relegated to a minor position. This is reflected in the small percentages which these e-publishing aspects received in comparison with the high percentages SNS received as a means of recreation and socialization. As to the fears and dangers arising from the usage of SNS, they were reported to be similar to those encountered or expressed by users of different background nationalities, where a number of dangers were listed, the most important of which are lack of privacy, security risks, and identity theft.

Keywords Social media · SNS usage · E-publishing · Online addiction · E-books

R.F. Hussein (✉)
Faculty of Foreign Languages, The University of Jordan, Amman, Jordan
e-mail: RHUSSEIN@ju.edu.jo

N. Taha et al. (eds.), *Social Media Shaping e-Publishing and Academia*,
DOI 10.1007/978-3-319-55354-2_7

1 Introduction

In the 1980s websites operated on Web 1.0 technologies where the text and graphics were mainly featured as static content and hosts were the primary content contributors and online information targeted a mostly passive audience that received rather than contributed content. In 1991 Web 2.0 was introduced which is characterized by the following features: free classification of information (folksonomy) which allows every user to create free classification and arrangement of information; rich user experience—unlike Web 1.0, Web 2.0, presents a dynamic rich experience to the site owner; in Web 2.0, however, the user is not passive as he/she can contribute to the content; long tail, where the service is negotiable and can either be approved or turned down; user participation, where users have the chance to participate in content sourcing; basic trust—in Web 1.0 contents are protected but in Web 2.0 they are shared, exchanged, and made available to everyone; and finally, dispersion—in Web 1.0 services are delivered directly to customers or users, while Web 2.0 delivery uses multiple channels.

Yim and Shin [10] define Web 2.0 as "the movement of opening information, through which services and platforms facilitate information sharing and voluntary participation within communities, which increases the value of information" (P. 3). One of the common characteristics of Web 2.0 services is strong user interaction. Web 2.0 services such as social networking sites (SNS), tagging, blogs, and RSS facilitate user interaction [7]. Furthermore, Yim and Shin explain the interconnectedness of Web 2.0 with other services:

> "to be successful in the market, Web 2.0 services require both active user interaction and well-designed systems accommodating them. For example, many web sites and blogs have an interconnective function like RSS, SNS, Twitter and so on. In order to support user interaction, Web 2.0 services should be interconnected seamlessly with other services so that users do not feel inconvenienced in utilizing other services' content. This means that Web 2.0 services should have compatibility with other Web 2.0 services." P. 2.

Thus, one very important implication of Web2.0 for social networking is that it has facilitated using SNS because of interconnectedness and interactivity. The different components of Web 2.0 have helped create and sustain social networks in different areas such as blogging, wikis, and file sharing or podcasting.

A social networking site is a web that enables users to create public profiles to form relationships with other users who access their profiles. Boyd and Ellison [1] define social network sites as "web–based services that allow individuals to (1) construct a public or semi public profile within a bounded system, (2) articulate a list of other users with whom they share a connection, and (3) view and traverse their list of connections and those made by others within the system. The nature and nomenclature of these connections may vary from site to site" (2007, p. 78).

Furthermore, social media is defined by Bryer and Zavattaro [2] as "technologies that facilitate social interaction, make possible collaboration, and enable deliberation across stakeholders. These technologies include blogs, wikis, media (audio, photo, video, text) sharing tools, networking platforms (including Facebook), and virtual worlds" (p. 11).

Buettner [3] suggests that "a social networking service is a platform to build social networks or social relations among people who share interests, activities, backgrounds or real-life connections. A social network service consists of a representation of each user (often a profile), his social links, and a variety of additional services". Deb Roy and Chakraborty [4] maintain that "social networking is one of the technological foundations of Web 2.0 which allows people to create, share, exchange information and ideas in virtual communication networks" (p. 215).

Social networking sites provide interactive platforms as envisioned by their founders. There are different platforms and each responds or caters to the needs and interests of certain individuals who are primarily interested in social, political, academic, cultural, or business affairs.

With regard to the types of social media, networking websites are the most popular form of social media; many types of online platforms can be classified under social media which include social networking sites, visual social networks, web blogs, and finally micro blogs. Social networking sites allow users to create web pages featuring personal information and interests. Subsequently, these pages enable users to connect with friends and family members, to share photos, video clips, and blogs; visual social networks differ from social networking sites because users can attach an image with their posts as in Twitter and Instagram. The ability to upload an image is making these networks extremely popular especially among the young and teenagers. Web blog is a web site in which writers express their opinions or observations on public matters or problems or on personal experience. There are different types of blogs which reflect different groups' interests which are related to politics, social matters, global warming, language learning, cooking, fashion, obesity, intermarriage, societal violence, quality of education abroad, travel, drug addiction, and so on. In blogs the entries can be arranged in a chronological or reverse chronological order where the oldest posts are listed first and the newest last as in Blogger and Tumblr. Finally, microblogs are blogging tools that feature short posts, which stand in contrast to journal-style posts. Users are usually allowed to post a few lines of text, or upload individual images and videos. Microblogging is mostly used for posting quick news and distributing content via mobile devices. In addition to Twitter and Tumblr, the well-known microblogging sites, other social networks such as Facebook, Google+, and Linkedin also have their own microblogging features and can be used for microblogging.

SNS are appealing to nearly all adults, teenagers, males, and females for a multitude of reasons, the most important of which are staying in touch with friends and family members; connecting with old friends and finding new ones who share similar interests or hobbies; posting comments; reading blogs posted by friends, acquaintances, political figures, celebrities, authorities in business and academia; discussing class assignments with fellow students; passing time; and finding suitable dating partners from the other gender. Ezumah [6] explicates that while the majority of SNS are viewed as a platform for socialization, learning orientation, content creation, and sharing and maintaining filial and casual relationships, others like LinkedIn are restricted to use for business and professional purposes. Ezumah asserts that "additional purposes included updating personal information and activities and maintaining a one-way parasocial relationship as in Twitter" (2013, p. 27).

Ezumah adds that "there is a natural nexus, of course, between media and technology. The trend in emergent technologies comprises three major components, namely: content creation, content sharing and connectivity. These are the attributes shared by social media, a phenomenon that now dominates most adult peoples' lives" (2013, p. 27). Facebook is the platform which is the most popular among all social networking sites and is gaining more and more popularity by the hour. This is shown by the fact that the number of monthly active Facebook users worldwide increased from a little more than 1 billion in the third quarter of 2012 to 1.55 billion monthly users in the third quarter of 2015. Active users are defined as those who have logged into Facebook during the last 30 days. Furthermore, as of that quarter, the biggest social networking service Facebook was also accessible to mobile web users and had 1.31 billion mobile monthly active users.

When 'The Facebook' was first launched in 2004, 1,200 Harvard students had signed up within 24 hours, and one month later, nearly half of the undergraduate students had a profile; then it began to spread worldwide, reaching UK universities the following month. Initially, the use of Facebook was restricted to the student population at Harvard but in September 2006, the network was extended beyond educational institutions and was available to anyone with a registered email address.

Despite the fact that people nowadays use a limited number of popular, social networking sites which are extensively used such as Twitter, Linkedin, and Google+, the fact of the matter is that there are hundreds of networking sites which were launched for general or specialized use as early as 1997 such as Sixdegrees and CarnigBridge; the latter was founded for no profit, providing free websites that connect family and friends during a serious health event, care, and recovery with 9,500,000 members.

Sixdegrees is a collection of websites that connect family and friends with nine and a half million subscribers was launched in 1997. In addition, Habbo was founded in 2008 for teenagers to communicate with one another with 268 million followers; Last fm was founded in 2002 for music fans and allowed the 30 million followers to discuss music-related issues and listen to a variety of music; MyLife made it possible for friends and family to locate one another with 51 million followers; Sina Weibo launched in 2009 for social microblogging with 300 million Chinese users; and finally Influenster launched in 2010 for online product sampling with 850,000 fans. This is in addition to scores of dating social networking sites online.

2 Statement of Problem

The use of social media is appealing to adults and teenagers of both sexes for many reasons, so this research attempts to explore why people continue to take a keen interest in social media and constantly use it. In addition, the use of SNS is linked to many problems and it is sometimes abused by users thus resulting in some grave dangers especially to young people and teenagers. Some students and teenagers are obsessed with the use of SNS to the extent that they use their mobiles to browse their Facebook or Twitter accounts when crossing a busy street which constitutes a risk of real physical harm. Conversely, they are not so keen on e-publishing usage such as e-books, e-blogging, online newspapers, and the digital library. This study therefore attempts to explore students' behavioral patterns as to the use of SNS and e-publishing and the dangers, if any that are associated with the former.

3 Objectives and Methodology

As stated above the major objectives of this research were to assess and survey various issues related to SNS, namely (a) use of social networking sites such as Facebook, Twitter, Instagram, Snapchat, Google+, and Linkedin; (b) e-publishing usage such as e-blogs, e-books, electronic journals, online newspapers, and the digital library; and finally (c) the dangers associated with using SNS as viewed by a sample of undergraduate students. More specifically, this chapter attempts to answer the following three questions:

1. To what extent do Jordanian undergraduate students use social networking sites? What do they use them for?
2. To what extent do Jordanian undergraduate students use e-publishing such as e-books, e-journals, online newspapers, and the digital library? What do they use them for?
3. What are the risks associated with using social networking sites as perceived by the students?

For this purpose a three-section questionnaire was developed by the researcher. The first part elicited demographic data such as age, gender, level, major, and faculty; the second part consisted of 12 questions, addressing issues related to primary social networks, purpose of using the social networking sites, time spent online and on SNS; the third part consisted of 12 questions aimed primarily to elicit data on e-publishing in general and e-books, e-blogging, e-journals, online newspapers, and finally the university digital library usage. Before administering the questionnaire, it was piloted and modified in light of the comments received from 36 students in the applied English program. Finally, the data obtained was tabulated on computer sheets and means and frequencies were calculated.

4 The Sample

The sample consisted of 260 respondents enrolled in the University of Jordan, Faculty of Foreign languages and King Abdullah II School for Information Technology (henceforth IT) in the first semester 2015/2016. More specifically, 140 participants from the Applied English program (henceforth AE) affiliated with the department of linguistics and 120 respondents from King Abdulla II School for Information Technology, 68 from the department of Computer Information Systems (CIS), and 52 from the Computer Science department comprised the sample. Originally, 300 questionnaires were distributed to respondents but 40 were excluded because of incomplete responses or missing information or patterned responding. In the AE group 127 (90.7%) female students in comparison with only 13 or 9.3% male subjects filled out the questionnaires. In the IT group 80 (66.7%) female students took part in comparison with 40 (33.3%) male respondents. The overall sample comprised 207 female and 53 male respondents. Females made up 79.6% and males 20.4% of the sample. This nearly reflects the female–male student ratio which in the Faculty of Foreign language is about 91% and in the Faculty of IT is 55.2%.

All participants are in the age group (19–22). For the sake of convenience entire classes in the AE program and departments of computer information systems and computer science were randomly selected but with proportionally greater selection from the AE program. Fifty-seven percent of the respondents are in the third year and 43% are either sophomores or juniors.

5 Results and Discussion

The results of this research are reported and discussed under three main subheadings: extent of use of SNS by university students; extent of e-publishing usage; and finally dangers associated with SNS usage as perceived by the sample.

6 Extent of SNS Usage

This section addresses the number of hours respondents spend online and on social network sites and the reasons why they use the social network sites. Item one in the questionnaire elicited data on the time respondents spend online each week: 21.5% said that they spend 26 h or more; 15.8% said they spend 21–25 h; 14.6% spend 16–20 h; 19.6% spend 11–15; 17.3% spend 6–10 h; and finally 11.2% spend 1–5 h. When asked about the number of hours they spend on social networks each week, 23% said they spend 26 h or more, 11.5% said they spend 21–25 h, 21% said 16–20 h, 18% said 11–15 h, 16.9% said 6–10 h, and finally 8.8% said 1–5 h as

Table 1 Number of weekly hours respondents spend online and on SNS

	%	Online	%	Social networks
1	21.5	More than 26	23.5	More than 26
2	15.8	21–25	11.5	21–25
3	14.6	16–20	21	16–20
4	19.6	11–15	18	11–15
5	17.3	6–10	16.9	6–10
6	11.2	1–5	8.8	1–5

shown in Table 1. These figures clearly show the great number of hours respondents spend on social networks and online and reflect their attachment to the Internet and to the social networks as well.

Table 1 clearly shows that more than 50% spend 16 h or more weekly online, whereas more than 55% spend more than 16 h weekly on the social network sites. This is almost equivalent to half the time an average employee or worker spends working in an office or shop to earn his/her living.

When asked about the primary social network for which they had created a profile, 192 or 80% said Facebook, 25 (12%) said WhatsApp, and the remaining 8% Snapchat, Instagram, and Google+. When asked about the number of followers or friends they have on their primary social network, about 64% indicated they have 121 followers or more, 15% had 91–120 followers, 7.3% had 61–90 followers, 9.6% had 31–60, and 4.2% had 1–30 followers. Little more than 13% had 60 or less friends or followers. Social network usage is of course proportional to the number of followers; that is, the more followers profile creators have, the more interaction occurs unidirectionally or bi-directionally.

Item five elicited data on how often respondents use their primary social network. 46.6% said 'always', 25% said 'often', 21.6% 'sometimes', 4.2% 'rarely', and 2.5% 'very rarely'. From the above, it is clear that an overwhelming majority (71%) said they 'always' or 'often' use SNS, in contrast to about 7% who use it 'rarely' and 'very rarely'. This unequivocally shows that a high percentage of respondents are hooked up to their social networking sites and are nearly always engaged in sending, downloading, socializing, and interacting with followers and friends.

Item six elicited data on the most important reasons why respondents use their primary social networks. AE respondents and IT respondents are in full agreement as to the ranking of the reasons, where staying in touch with friends and relatives ranked first, followed by socializing and having fun. Of least importance are killing time and playing games as shown in Table 2.

The lower ranking of the last two items in Table 2 is attributed to the fact that university students are inundated with too much academic work and preparing for exams conducting research and undertaking projects and so cannot afford the time to play games or waste valuable time. Deb Roy and Chakraborty stated that Facebook is the most popular site among youths; it provides individuals with a way of maintaining and strengthening social ties which can be beneficial to both social and academic settings. These same ties, however, also badly affect their "privacy,

Table 2 Means and ranking for the reason of SNS usage by the overall sample

	Applied English respondents		Information technology respondents	
Item	Mean	Ranking	Mean	Ranking
To stay in touch with friends	2.60	1	2.47	1
To socialize and have fun	3.11	2	3.10	2
To share photos, video clips	3.80	3	3.50	3
To interact with other students	3.90	4	3.60	4
To make new relations	4.30	5	4.20	5
To kill time	4.50	6	5.20	6
To play games	5.60	7	5.90	7

safety and focus of attention" (2008, p. 147). In line with this, Ezumah (2015) suggested that the active audience usage of mass media and SNS is directly related to the Gratification theory where people use specific media content to gratify some needs. He added that

> "Social networking sites are an appealing medium for various personal human gratifications, including but not limited to, staying in touch with current friends, staying in touch with family members, connecting with old friends, connecting with others who share similar hobbies and interests, reading comments by celebrities, athletes or politicians as well as finding potential romantic or dating partners." (2015, P. 27)

Item seven elicited data related to the use of the computer, the mobile or both to access their social networking sites. Two hundred and one, (77.3%) of the respondents, access their networks on their mobiles, whereas 27 (10.4%) on the computer, and 32 (12.3%) on both the computer and the mobile.

Items 8, 9, and 10 elicited data on whether the subjects have a Twitter account, and if so the number of followers they have on the site and finally how often they tweet to their friends or followers. Item 8 elicited data as to whether respondents have a Twitter account or not. Forty-six (32.8%) of the AE and 48 (40%) of the IT respondents said they have a Twitter account. As to the number of followers they have on their accounts, 16.6% of the AE respondents said they have 150 followers or more, 8.3% said 120–150, 5% said 91–120, 12 5% 61–90, 16.6% 31–60, and finally 37.7% 1–30 followers; whereas the number of IT followers was as follows: 15.7% said they have 150 followers or more; 6.9% said 121–150; 13.8% said 91–120; 22.4% said 61–90; 10.3% said 31–60; and finally 31% said 1–30.

Item 10 elicited data related to the frequency of tweeting on Twitter; 13.7% of the AE respondents said 'always'; 16% said 'often'; 28% said 'sometimes'; 35% said 'rarely'; and 8.4% said 'very rarely'. This in comparison with 10.3% of the IT respondents who said 'always', 55.2% said 'often', 20.7% said 'sometimes', 10.3% 'rarely', and finally 3.4% 'very rarely'.

Item 11 elicited data related to the other social networks for which AE and IT respondents had created a personal profile. The frequencies of the most popular sites are shown in Table 3.

Table 3 Frequency of other SNS for which respondents created a personal profile

	AE respondents	IT respondents	Total
WhatsApp	61	35	96
Instagram	43	48	91
Twitter	40	48	88
Snapchat	51	28	79
YouTube	20	02	22
Google+	12	10	22
Pinterest	10	03	13
Linkedin	6	05	11
Yahoo	8	02	10

Table 1 clearly shows that in addition to the primary social networking site, Facebook and other sites are popular but are not as popular among the sample: WhatsApp with a frequency of 96; Instagram 91; Twitter 88; and Snapchat 79. This of course reflects the popularity of these sites worldwide.

The section on SNS usage clearly shows that the respondents are strongly attached to online and social networking sites as they spend so many hours navigating or browsing these media. It was also shown that a good number of respondents had created an account on at least one of the primary social networking sites. In addition, some indicated they use other social networking sites, mainly WhatsApp, Instagram, Snapchat, and YouTube. Respondents also indicated that they use social networking sites mainly for staying in touch with friends and relatives and socializing and having fun. Killing time and playing games, however, were shown to be the least important reasons for using social media.

7 Extent of E-Publishing Usage

In the questionnaire, 12 questions were designed to elicit responses of direct relevance to e-publishing, such as blogs, e-books, e-journals, e-newspapers, and the university digital library. Item 13 elicited data related to whether respondents have a blogging page and how often they blog and finally whether they read other people's blogs. Of the AE respondents, only 27 or (19.2%) in comparison to 22 (18.3%) of the IT respondents said they have a blogging page. As to how often they blog, 14.8% of the AE respondents said 'always', 22.2% said 'often', 33.3% said 'sometimes', and 29.6% said 'rarely'; whereas 18.2% of the IT respondents said 'always', 4.5% said 'often', 31.8% said 'sometimes', and 45.4% said 'rarely'. Item 15 elicited data as to whether respondents read other people's blogs; 19 (13.5%) AE respondents and only eight (6.6%) of the IT respondents said that they do.

Item 16 elicited data related to e-books usage. Forty-four (31%) of the AE respondents said they use e-books in comparison with 42 (35%) of the IT respondents. The relatively low use of e-books does not seem to be peculiar to the Jordanian respondents. Rosenita and Zainab [8] reported that "the level of e -book uses among the students is still low. The reasons for this are clearly related to preference for the printed format and lack of knowledge of its use" (p. 18). With regard to the types of books they use, 12 (28.6%) of the AE respondents said textbooks, 14 (33.3%) said dictionaries, 6 (14%) said references, 2 (4.5%) said fiction, and 8 (18.2%) said a combination of the above. Eight (14.3%) of the IT respondents said textbooks, 10 (23.8%) said dictionaries, 14 (33.3%) said references, 6 (14.3%) said fiction, and 4 (9.5%) said a combination of the above. When asked how often they use e-books, 5 AE respondents (11.4%) said 'always', 9 (20.4%) said 'often', 16 (36.4%) said 'sometimes', and 14 (31.8%) said 'rarely'; by comparison, 6 (14.3.%) of the IT respondents said 'always', 12 (28.6%) said 'often', 11 (26.2%) said 'sometimes', and 13 (30.9%) said 'rarely'.

Item 19 elicited data related to the usage of e-journals. Fifty-eight (41.4%) out of 140 AE respondents said they use e-journals in comparison with 35 or (29.2%) of the IT respondents. Out of the 58 AE respondents, 8 (13.8%) said 'always', 20 (34.4%) said 'often', 24 (41.3%) said 'sometimes', and 6 or (10.3%) said 'rarely'; whereas 3 (8.5%) of the IT respondents said 'always', 11 (31.4%) said 'often', 13 or (37.1%) said 'sometimes', and 8 (22.8%) said 'rarely'.

Item 21 elicited data on the usage of online newspapers. Sixty-four (45%) out of the AE respondents said they use online newspapers in comparison with 47 (39.2%) of the IT. When asked how often they use online newspapers 18 (28%) of the AE respondents said 'always', 14 (21.8%) said 'often', 20 (31.2%) said 'sometimes', and 12 (18.7%) said 'rarely'; while 15 (31.9%) of the IT respondents said 'always', 9 (19.2%) said 'often', seven (14.8%) said 'sometimes', and 16 (34%) said 'rarely'.

Item 23 deals with the use of the university digital library. Thirty-six (25.7%) of the AE respondents said they use the digital library in comparison with 41 (34.2%) of the IT respondents. Item 24 elicited data on how often respondents use the digital library. Four (11.1%) of the AE said 'always', 5 (13.8%) said 'often', 7 (19.4%) said 'sometimes', 13 (36.1%) said 'rarely', and 7 (19.4%) said 'never; while 7 (17%) of the IT respondents said 'always', 5 (12.2%) said 'often', 8 (19.5%) said 'sometimes', 10 (24.4%) said 'rarely', and 11 (26.8%) said 'never'.

Unlike using social networking sites, e-publishing in all its aspects does not seem to be so popular amongst the respondents as a relatively small number or respondents use this service. For instance approximately 20% of the whole sample indicated that they have a blogging page and even a smaller percentage of the AE respondents (13.5%) and 6.6% of the IT respondents said they read other people's blogs. With regard to reading e-books, about one-third (31%) of the AE respondents and (35%) of the IT respondents indicated that they use e-books. One explanation for the unpopularity of e-books can be attributed to a number of factors, the most important of which is the high cost and lack of technological know-how. In addition, e-books may be tiring for the eyes and the brain. Finally, as indicated by Rosenita and Zainab, (2005) the unpopularity may be related to preference for the printed format and lack of knowledge of e-books use.

With regard to e-journals, a relatively higher percentage of AE respondents (41.4%) in comparison with 29.2% of the IT respondents said they use e-journals. College students in general should be encouraged to use e-journals due to ease of downloading to personal computers, and due to 24 h accessibility and speed of access and searching, and finally their importance in academic research.

The results showed about only one-third of the sample use the digital library and only 24% of the AE respondents use it 'always' or 'often', compared to 29% of the IT respondents who use it 'always' or 'often'. Little more than 70% or so use the digital library 'rarely' or 'never'. This clearly shows that undergraduate students rarely make use of the university digital library perhaps because of a poor understanding of the services that are offered there and because university instructors do not seem to emphasize the role of the digital library as a medium of learning and research.

8 Dangers Associated with SNS Usage

Item 12 was devised to elicit data of direct relevance to the dangers associated with SNS usage, and respondents were asked to rank them from one to seven, one being the most dangerous and seven the least dangerous; it follows that the smaller the mean, the more dangerous the item. The mean of responses in Table 4 indicates that the AE and IT respondents agreed on ranking lack of privacy first, security risk and identity theft second, and addiction third. But whereas AE respondents ranked exposure to pornography fourth (4.3), and sexual exploitation fifth (4.5), the IT respondents reversed the order. Both groups, however, agreed on ranking laziness and health problems last as shown in Table 4. In their research on Internet addiction, Vijay, Chellavel, Duraimurugan Abirami, and Reji found that (41.3%) of the

Table 4 Means and ranking of dangers associated with SNS as viewed by the sample

	Applied English respondents		Information Technology respondents	
Item	Mean	Ranking	Mean	Ranking
Lack of privacy	2.7	1	2.6	1
Security risk and identity	3.1	2	2.9	2
Addiction	3.8	3	4.0	3
Exposure to pornography	4.3	4	4.6	5
Sexual exploitation	4.5	5	4.2	4
Laziness	4.6	6	4.8	6
Health problems	4.9	7	5.3	7

students were mild addicts, (15.2%) were moderate addicts, and (43.5%) were not addicted to the Internet use at all and there was no pattern of severe Internet addiction among the study group. Although this study was conducted on their use of the Internet, implications can be drawn for SNS usage. It is evident therefore that the majority of respondents are aware of the potential dangers of social networking sites. In addition to these dangers, there may be others which are as serious or even more serious.

Eke et al. [5] listed a number of drawbacks related to social networking sites, namely sharing too much information; illusion of familiarity; and predators and stalkers. Users can lose a lot through leaking information on social networking. "Even if a user of a social site has her privacy settings of highest level, the information can still be passed on by someone on their friends list" [5, p. 10]. This information can be used for potential crimes such as identity theft or fraud. Also SNS can create the illusion of familiarity and intimacy and users may be inclined to share information which should have been kept private. Hackers or predators could easily steal teenagers' identities subsequent to completing their online profile and giving away much of their personal information. Any of their 'friends' can have access to their full names, date of birth, and home address, and so hack their profile or steal their identity. So, despite the benefits associated with SNS, nevertheless this usage sometimes entails a host of fears or dangers which should be taken into account when people, especially teenagers, embark on downloading their profiles on one of the social networking sites.

9 Summary and Conclusion

This study is a preliminary step toward the identification of SNS and e-publishing usage as viewed by a sample of Jordanian University students. In addition, it aimed to reveal the dangers associated with SNS usage among them in the fall semester 2015/2016.

Analysis of the data indicated that Jordanian students are not unlike their counterparts in the US, Europe, Asia, or Africa in the sense that they are strongly attached not only to online communication and the Internet but also to social media, despite some shortcomings. This usage seems to create a new community parallel to the international community but with different aims, scope and orientation, where the spirit of cooperation, the desire to understand, accept, and respect others prevail among many SNS users. Constantly communicating with one another inevitably enforces and enhances all these positive qualities and bridges the gap between users from different background nationalities. Like their counterparts across the world, Jordanian respondents exhibited a strong attachment to SNS such as Facebook, Twitter, WhatsApp, Instagram, and Snapchat. Though Facebook has been shown to be far more popular than the other sites, a good percentage still uses the other SNS sites such as Twitter; more than 30% of the sample said they use it to connect with friends and the majority of them have more than 31 followers or 'friends'.

As a result of the sustained usage of SNS and due to good connectivity, not only has the number of followers on SNS increased but also the number of hours spent contacting friends, relatives, and downloading photos, videos, and video clips. An overwhelming majority said they 'always' or 'often' use SNS and this may lead to negative impact as mentioned by Deb Roy and Chakraborty [4] who stated that: "Facebook is the most popular site among youths; it provides individuals with a way of maintaining and strengthening social ties which can be beneficial to both social and academic settings. These same ties, however, also badly affect their privacy, safety and focus of attention" [4, p. 147]. Another danger associated with SNS is addiction, which is sometimes used to refer to someone spending too much time using different forms of social media—so much so that it interferes with other aspects of their daily life. The following quotation indicates how much SNSs have penetrated people's lives in Australia. It would not be unreasonable to say that the addiction rates may be the same or even higher in other industrial or developing countries.

> "A survey conducted in Australia on men and women aged between 16 and 25 years revealed certain startling facts. Sixty per cent of the surveyed population admitted that they checked their media feed 10 times a day. Even among them, there was a behavioural difference between different age groups. Those in the age group of 15–19 spend three hours a day, and of 20–29 spend two hours. The most shocking statistic is that 50 per cent of those surveyed admitted they were addicted and among those addicted 60 per cent were women. I am forced to use the word addiction here because they have admitted that they cannot live without accessing social media networks. These observations and inferences do not pertain to any particular country. It is global. People, particularly the youth, are hooked on to social media". The Indian Express 2013.

With regard to e-publishing, the findings showed a relatively small percentage of e-publishing usage, namely, blogging, e-books, e-journals, online newspapers, and the university digital library among both the AE and the IT groups. This finding is in contrast with SNS usage as a medium of recreation and socialization. What we would like to see is a reversal of the roles, where the functions of SNS as a learning medium exceed those of socialization.

The low usage of e-publishing can be attributed to a number of factors such as the large amount of time users spend on downloading photos, making new friends, and sharing videos and files; second, some teachers and students are still traditionally oriented and still view e-publishing as extraordinary and this entails using printed materials as the norm and electronic materials as the exception. Third, due to some constraints on downloading and accessing electronic texts, users may get disappointed due to a lack of technical know-how and consequently give up on accessing e-books, e-journals, and other electronic texts.

SNS usage, very much like modern technology, has its advantages and disadvantages; it has certainly made access to information easier, improved communication, increased efficiency, and has made it easier to discover new friends and connect with relatives and old friends, download videos and share files, read comments by politicians and celebrities, play games, and write and read blogs. The advantages, however, certainly outweigh the disadvantages, but we cannot turn a blind eye to them, as they are responsible for loneliness which is on the increase among the young and the old. It is also responsible for the breach of personal privacy and space, addiction, security risks and identity theft, laziness, and other health problems. SNS users should maximize the advantages and minimize the disadvantages by emphasizing more the use of e-publishing and the academic aspects of SNS such as e-books, e-journals, blogging, online newspapers, and the digital library.

To conclude, some recommendations are made which pertain to the research study's scope and purposes. First, research should be conducted on e-publishing usage among graduate students in different faculties such as arts, business, educational sciences, law, science, agriculture, engineering, pharmacy, dentistry, and nursing to see how their patterns of e-publishing usage differ from those of the undergraduate students in this study.

Second, a gender-based study on SNS addiction among college and high school students should be conducted to find out the variation of addiction behaviors among them and the best ways to deal with them. Finally, a study needs to be conducted on the potential dangers of SNS usage among high school students to see how they are different from those encountered by university students.

Questionnaire

This questionnaire aims to investigate social media and e-publishing usage among college students. The researcher assures you that the information obtained in response to the items of the questionnaire will be strictly confidential and used solely for the purpose of academic research and will be used only by the researcher.

It is hoped that you will cooperate by providing answers to the following questions. Thank you so much

The Researcher
Prof. Riyad F Hussein
Dept of linguistics
The University of Jordan

- Age _______
- Sex _______
- Major _______
- Level _______
- Faculty _______
- University _______

1. How many hours do you spend online each week?

- 1–5 h
- 6–10 h
- 11–15 h

- 16–20 h
- 21–25 h
- More than 26

2. How many hours do you spend on social networks each week?

- 1–5 h
- 6–10 h
- 11–15 h
- 16–20 h
- 21–25 h
- More than 26

3. What is the social network that you constantly use?
4. How many friends do you have on this network?

- 30
- 31–60
- 61–90
- 91–120
- 121–150
- 151 or more

5. How often do you use your primary social network?
Always often sometimes rarely very rarely
6. What do you use your primary social network for? Rank them according to importance from 1 to 7, 1 being the most important
a to stay in touch with family and friends ( )

a. to make new relations ( )
b. to socialize and have fun ( )
c. to kill time ( )
d. to play games ( )
e. to share photos, videos and video clips ( )
f. to interact with other students ( )

7. Do you access your primary social network on your mobile or computer?
8. Do you have a Twitter account? Please circle Yes or No
9. If yes, how many Twitter followers do you have?

- 1–30
- 31–60
- 61–90
- 91–120
- 121–150
- More than 151

10. How often do you tweet?
Always often sometimes rarely very rarely

11. What are the other social networks for which you have created a personal profile? Rank them from 1 to 3, 1 being the most important

1-
2-
3-

12. What in your opinion are the risks associated with using social networking sites (Rank them from 1 to 7, I being the most dangerous)

a. Exposure to pornography [ ]
b. Lack of privacy [ ]
c. Laziness [ ]
d. Addiction [ ]
e. Security risk and identity theft [ ]
f. Sexual exploitation [ ]
g. Health problems [ ]

13. Do you have a blogging page? Please circle Yes or No
14. If yes, how often do you blog?
Always often sometimes rarely never
15. Do you read other people's blogs? Please circle yes or No
16. Do you use e-books? Please circle Yes or No
17. If yes, what kinds of e-books do you use?
Textbooks, dictionaries references fiction others specify
18. How often do you use them?
Always often sometimes rarely never
19. Do you use e-journals? Please circle Yes or No
20. If yes, how often do you use them?
Always often sometimes rarely never
21. Do you use online newspapers? Please circle Yes or No
22. How often do you read these newspapers?
Always often sometimes rarely never
23. Do you use the digital library of the university? Please circle Yes or No
24. If yes, how often do you use it?
Always often sometimes rarely never
T h a n k y o u

References

1. Boyd D, Ellison N (2007) Social network sites: definition, history, and scholarship. J Comput Mediated Commun 13(1):210–230
2. Bryer TA, Zavattaro SM (2011) Social media and public administration: theoretical dimensions and introduction to the symposium. Adm Theory Praxis 33:325–340
3. Buettner R (2016) Getting a job via career-oriented social networking sites: the weakness of ties. In: 49th annual Hawaii international conference on system sciences. Kauai, Hawaii

4. Deb Roy S, Chakraborty S (2015) Impact of social media/social networks on education and life of undergraduate level students of Karimganj town-A survey. Int Res J Interdisc Multi Stud (IRJIMS) 1(2):141–147
5. Eke H, Omekwu C, Odoh J (2014) The use of social networking sites among the undergraduate students of University of Nigeria, Nsukka. Lit Philos Pract 1:1–27
6. Ezumah BA (2013) College students' use of social media: Site preferences, uses and gratifications theory revisited. Int J Bus Soc Sci 4(5):27–34
7. McLoughlin C and Lee M (2007) Social software and participatory learning: pedagogical choices with technology affordances in the Web 2.0 era. In: Proceedings Ascilite Singapore
8. Rosenita I, Zainab A (2005) The pattern of e-book use amongst undergraduate students in Malaysia. J Libr Inf Sci 2(1):1–23
9. Vijay AP, Ganapthi CR, Duraimurugan K, Abirami V, Reji E (2015) Internet addiction and associated factors: a study among college students' in South India. Int J Med Health Sci 3:121–125
10. Yim S and Shin M (Date) Effects of the Web.2.0 and social network services environment on information quality and intentions to reuse. A published research article on the internet supported by Korea communications commission (give access details)

Part III
Information Retrieval in Social Media

The exponential growth of data over the internet is increasing rapidly, where the internet is becoming part of everyone's life. Hence, it is important to know how we can use this huge data resource to access, analyze, and extract useful information that helps in changing several web factors including web usage, content, and structure. Investigating and designing new Information Retrieval (IR) models to include and measure this increase of information about Social Network Analysis (SNA) is needed. Moreover, since there is a huge availability of data over the internet, it is possible and applicable to find connections between different concepts of web behavioral data that allow us finally to automatically generate and extract useful information.

The authors of the first chapter developed a defeasible description logic system that can represent a flexible publication ontology which can support intelligent queries. Their system uses the description of the logical system ALC to build the ontology. They extend an ALC knowledge base with defeasible rules to yield a defeasible description logic system called Def-ALC. This system (Def-ALC) is useful to users of a digital library and will be flexible and decidable. On the other hand, the authors mention that it is important to have complete information in a decidable manner for description logic or defeasible logic to be suitable for reasoning. They have made a first step towards developing fully defeasible description logic by implementing a prototype of a publication ontology Def-ALC. Finally, the authors state that a more thorough study and comparison with other systems that employ knowledge base implementation using description logic is needed.

In the second chapter, the authors have developed a retrieval method that can meet users' requests and handle the diversity of them by investigating several techniques to support users in searching and navigating the full texts of digitized books and complementary social media in order to enhance the user book search experience. They used the INEX SBS track which uses professional metadata and user-generated metadata (social media content) to enhance the retrieval process of books by optimizing simple search query, where extracting relevant topics that are related to book searching is done using the Named Entity Recognition tagger (NER) and the Part-Of-Speech tagger (POS). Their results state that using NER and POS tagging can generate a very effective query for book retrieval.

Ali Rodan

A Defeasible Description Logic for Representing Bibliographic Data

Ala'a Al-Shaikh, Hebatallah Khattab, Asma Moubaiddin and Nadim Obeid

Abstract In this chapter, we make a first step toward developing a defeasible description logic system that can represent a flexible publication ontology which can support intelligent queries. It involves using the description logic system *ALC* to build the ontology. We extend an *ALC* knowledge base with defeasible rules to yield a defeasible description logic system called *Def-ALC*. *Def-ALC* will be useful to users of a digital library and will be flexible and decidable. We shall show that a superiority relation between rules gives us a ranking of the rules which could be beneficial as it can be adjusted to meet the needs of various users and user groups. A prototype of a publication ontology is developed and implemented using *Def-ALC*.

Keywords Description logic · Defeasible logic · Nonmonotonic · Ontology

1 Introduction

Recently, DIGital Libraries (DIGL) [1] have emerged as a powerful alternative to traditional libraries in terms of providing maintenance and easy access to published material. However, the published material has to be represented in digital form. The ease of access is facilitated by the use of metadata which supports information retrieval. It will be useful to users, say researchers, if they can make more intelligent queries such as: return the publications on a particular topic or subtopic (e.g., algorithms) in the past 2 years or return the name of researchers who are active in a particular research area. Answering such queries requires nonambiguous and concise knowledge about concepts such as publication and researcher and about the relationships between these concepts. Such knowledge can be represented using

A. Al-Shaikh · H. Khattab · N. Obeid (✉)
King Abdullah II School for Information Technology, The University of Jordan, Amman, Jordan
e-mail: obein@ju.edu.jo

A. Moubaiddin
Faculty of Foreign Languages, The University of Jordan, Amman, Jordan

N. Taha et al. (eds.), *Social Media Shaping e-Publishing and Academia*,
DOI 10.1007/978-3-319-55354-2_8

ontologies. An ontology is a model of organized knowledge in a restricted domain. Ontologies represent knowledge on the semantic level. They contain semantic entities (e.g., concepts, relations, attributes, and instances) and they allow specifying semantic relations between entities and axioms about a knowledge domain. Ontologies, together with annotations, allow us to organize available documents, resolve authorization conflicts, and control access to needed document contents. Researchers have made some attempts to use ontologies in DIGL [2] and in using annotation of published material [3] to allow easy access to published material.

A description logic [4] is mainly used to represent and reason about the conceptual knowledge of a domain. It allows us to define concepts of the domain as formulae in "First-Order Predicate Calculus (FOPC)." It has a model theory (Sematics) and it allows us to make inferences from the explicit knowledge which is contained in a Knowledge Base (KB) of a domain. Description logic systems are used as the logical formalisms for ontologies and the Semantic Web. Some of the important features of description logic systems are that: (1) the core reasoning problems are (usually) decidable; and (2), efficient decision procedures have been designed and implemented for these problems. This explains why most ontologies are represented using description logic.

Approaches which employ FOPC assume complete knowledge and they suffer from not being able to deal with inconsistency. When an inconsistency arises in a KB, then every conclusion can be derived and the system collapses. However, available knowledge is usually incomplete and uncertain. Defeasible/default logic [5–15] is appropriate in those situations, where we have only partial knowledge of the actual state of affairs. Nonmonotonic rule systems offer more expressive capabilities and are closer to commonsense reasoning. There are many scenarios in which conflicting rules may arise on the Web or in the context of DIGL such as: (1) reasoning with incomplete information; (2) rules with exceptions; (3) default inheritance in ontologies; and (4) ontology merging.

In this chapter, we make a first step toward developing a defeasible description logic system that can represent a flexible publication ontology which can support intelligent queries. It involves using the description logic system *ALC* to build the ontology. It also involves the addition of defeasible rules to an *ALC* knowledge base to achieve a flexible and decidable reasoning system called *Def-ALC* which can be useful to users of a digital library. However, the question of how to determine the priority between the defeasible rules is essential. There are many possible ways to proceed; one possibility would be to leave it to the experts in the domain; another possibility would be employ preferential models such that the rules which defeat as few as possible of the axioms of the KB are preferred. A prototype of a publication ontology is developed and implemented using *Def-ALC*.

In Sect. 2 we present the description logic system *ALC*. In Sect. 3, we present Defeasible Logic (*DefL*). In Sect. 4, we present Defeasible ALC (*Def-ALC*) which combines both *ALC* and *DefL*. In Sect. 5, we employ an example of a publication ontology to show some of the features of *Def-ALC*. In Sect. 6, we present a discussion of some relevant work. In Sect. 7, we present a concluding remark together with some indications for future work.

2 Description Logic: *ALC*

ALC has two basic notions: concepts which can be represented as unary predicates and roles which are represented as binary relations in FOPC. We shall use $P, P_1, \ldots Cp_1, Cp_2, \ldots$ for concept names, $R_0, R_1, \ldots$ for role names, a, b, c ... for object names, and A, B, C, ... for propositional variables. ALC provides us with the following constructors: negation ($\neg$), conjunction ($\prod$), existential ($\exists$), and universal ($\forall$) restriction.

Let T (resp. $\perp$) denotes the universal (resp. bottom) concept. Atomic concepts are concepts. Complex concepts are formed in a way similar to that of well-formed formulae in FOPC. That is, if P is an atomic concept then $\neg$P is a concept. If R is a role and Cp, Cp_1, and Cp_2 are concepts then $\forall$R.P and $\exists$R.T are concepts.

It is important to note that only the universal concept T is allowed in the scope of $\exists$R.

As mentioned in Sect. 1, *ALC* has a model theoretic semantics. Let I stand for an interpretation and Dom^I denote the domain of I. I is a function that assigns to every atomic concept P a set $P^I \subseteq Dom^I$ and to every atomic role R a binary relation $R^I \subseteq Dom^I \times Dom^I$. I can be extended to more complex concepts using the following definitions:

$$T^I = \Delta^I, \perp^I = \emptyset, (\neg Cp)^I = Dom^I \backslash Cp^I, (Cp_1 \prod Cp_2)^I = Cp_1^I \cap Cp_2^I$$
$$(\forall R.Cp)^I = \{\alpha \in Dom^I | \forall \beta.(\alpha, \beta) \in R^I \rightarrow \beta \in Cp^I\}$$
$$(\exists R.T)^I = \{\alpha \in Dom^I | \exists \beta.(\alpha, \beta) \in R^I\}$$

An *ALC* Knowledge Base (*ALC-KB*) is composed of two parts: T-Box and A-Box. T-Box contains general knowledge about a domain. Such knowledge is expressed as axioms about relations among concepts and/or roles which are essential for defining complex concepts from existing ones. A T-Box axiom may take one of the following forms:

$$(A \times 1)\, Cp_1 \sqsubseteq Cp_2 \quad (A \times 2)\, R_1 \sqsubseteq R_2$$
$$(A \times 3)\, Cp_1 \equiv Cp_2 \quad (A \times 4)\, R_1 \equiv R_2$$

Note that '$\sqsubseteq$' is called a strict subsumption relation between concepts and/or roles. '$\equiv$' is the equality relation between concepts and/or roles. '$\equiv$' can be defined in terms of '$\sqsubseteq$' as follows: $Cp_1 \equiv Cp_2$ is equivalent to $Cp_1 \sqsubseteq Cp_2$ and $Cp_2 \sqsubseteq Cp_1$.

Let A be a proposition. We shall employ $I \models A$ to mean I satisfies A. For instance,

$$I \models Cp_1 \sqsubseteq Cp_2 \text{ If } Cp_1^I \subseteq Cp_2^I \text{ and}$$
$$I \models Cp_1 \equiv Cp_2 \text{ if } Cp_1^I \subseteq Cp_2^I \text{ and } Cp_2^I \subseteq Cp_1^I.$$

The A-Box, which stands for assertional box, is used to describe a specific state of affairs related to a domain. An A-Box contains assertions of the form $\alpha : CP$ and $(\alpha, \beta) : R$.$\alpha : Cp$ is a concept assertion. It states that the individual α belongs to the concept Cp. That is, $I \models \alpha : Cp$ if $\alpha^I \in Cp^I$. $(\alpha, \beta) :$ R is a role assertion. $I \models (\alpha, \beta) : R$ if $(\alpha^I, \beta^I) \in R^I$

3 Defeasible Logic (*DefL*)

DefL [15] is a nonmonotonic logic based on the use of logical rules and priorities between them. It is simple, efficient, flexible, and capable of dealing with many nonmonotonic reasoning aspects. Furthermore, a semantic account based on argumentation can be provided for *DefL* [16]. Some studies show that *DefL* is appropriate for reasoning in various applications such as societies of agents, contracts, Semantic Web, and legal reasoning [17].

The language of L_{DefL} has connectives &, $\vee$, $\rightarrow$, $\Rightarrow$, and $\neg$. The $\rightarrow$ (resp. $\Rightarrow$) represents the classical (resp. defeasible) implication and $\leftrightarrow$ represents the classical logic equivalence. For propositions A and B, $A \Rightarrow B$ represents a defeasible implication and $A \sim\sim> B$ represents a defeater. Defeaters do not directly sanction drawing conclusions but they can block the application of some defeasible rules.

Definite and Defeasible Proofs

Let R be a rule and $B \in L_{DefL}$. We employ Ant(R) to represent the set of well-formed formula (WFF) that occur in the antecedent of R and Conseq(R) for its consequent. Let K be a set of rules. We partition K into three subsets: K_s to designate strict rules, K_d to designate defeasible rules, and K_{dft} to denote defeaters in K. Let $K_{sd} = K_s \cup K_d$. Let K[B] refers to the set of rules in K that has B as a consequent.

We define a defeasible theory DT as a tuple (KB, $\geq$) where KB = $\langle F, K \rangle$ such that F refers to a finite set of facts, K refers to a finite set of rules, and $\geq$ is a preference relation on K. Let S-Provable stands for provable using facts and strict rules and Def-Provable stands for defeasibly provable where in the proof of proposition we may employ propositions with defeasible implication $\Rightarrow$. An inference from KB is a labeled literal that takes one of the following forms as presented in [18]: (1) $+\Delta B$: B is D-Provable, (2) $-\Delta B$: B is not D-Provable, (3) $+\delta B$: B is Def-Provable and (4) $-\delta B$: B is not Def-Provable.

In the remaining part of this section, we shall present $+\Delta B$ and $+\delta B$. $-\Delta B$ and $-\delta B$ can easily be defined by negating every clause in $+\Delta B$ and $+\delta B$, respectively. A proof is a finite sequence $P_n = (P(1), \ldots, P(n))$ of labeled WFF as mentioned above. Let P(1..i) denote the first i items of a proof of length n, where $i < n$.

$$+\Delta : \text{If } P(i+1) = +\Delta B \text{ then}$$

(1) $B \in F$ or
(2) $(\exists R1 \in K_s[B])(\forall A \in Ant(R_1) : +\Delta A \in P(1..i))$.

The definition of Δ is the standard definition of forward chaining of strict inference rules. B is D-Provable if there is an $R_1 \in K_s$ such that $Conseq(R_1) = B$ and every member of Ant(R1) is D-Provable.

$+\delta$: If $P(i+1) = +\delta B$ then either
(1) $+\Delta B \in P(1..i)$ or
(2) (2.1) $(\exists R1 \in K_{sd}[B])(\forall A \in Ant(R_1) : +\delta a \in P(1..i)$ and
(2.2) $(-\Delta\neg B \in P\ (1..i))$ and
(2.3) $(\forall R1 \in K[\neg B])$ either
(2.3.1) $((\exists A \in Ant(R_1) : -\delta A \in P(1..i))$ or
(2.3.2) $((\exists R_2 \in K_{sd}[B])$ such that $R_2 > R_1$ and $(\forall A \in Ant(R_2) : +\delta A \in P(1..i))$

The idea is as follows: To show that B is Def-Provable, there are two choices: either (1) show that B is S-Provable; or (2) makes use of K_d. This requires us to perform one of the following three steps: (2.1) find an applicable rule in K_{sd} that has B as a consequent; (2.2) show that ¬B is not S-Provable; or (2.3) counterattack each rule that attacks the conclusion B by a stronger rule that supports B.

4 Defeasible *ALC* (*Def-ALC*)

This section is with concerned with extending *ALC* with defeasible rules. As mentioned above, *ALC* is monotonic where the A-Box captures the true facts that describe a state of affairs and the T-Box expresses the relations among concepts and/or roles.

Let α, β denote individuals, P be an atomic concept, R be a role, Cp, Cp_1, and Cp_2 denote concepts. We define a translation τ that takes element the A-Box and T-Box of a knowledge base into the language of a defeasible theory as follows:

1. $\tau(\alpha) = \alpha'$
2. $\tau(p) = p'$
3. $\tau(R) = R'$
4. $\tau(\alpha{:}Cp) = \tau(Cp)(\tau(\alpha))$
5. $\tau((\alpha, \beta){:}\ R) = \tau(R)(\tau(\alpha),\tau(\beta))$
6. $\tau(Cp_1 \sqsubseteq Cp_2) = (\tau(Cp_1) \rightarrow \tau(Cp_2))$
7. $\tau(Cp_1 \prod Cp_2) = \tau(Cp_1)\ \&\ \tau(Cp_2)$

Nonmonotonicity requires us to define a defeasible subsumption relation between concepts $\precsim$ such that $\tau(Cp_1 \precsim Cp_2) = (\tau(Cp_1) \Rightarrow \tau(Cp_2))$ where $\Rightarrow$ is the defeasible implication. We may define $\geq$ as a binary superiority relation between the defeasible rules.

Let Dom denote the domain of the theory and INDIV stands for the set of all individuals occurring in the assertions in A-Box. We are now in a position to give the conditions required for the strict and defeasible derivation of new role restrictions.

Strict derivation:

$$+\Delta\forall R.Cp : \text{If } P(i+1) = +\forall R.Cp(\alpha) \text{ then } \forall\beta \in \text{INDIV either}$$

(1) $-\Delta R(\alpha, \beta)$ or
(2) $+\Delta Cp(\beta)$

Defeasible derivation:

$$+\delta\forall R.Cp : \text{If } P(i+1) = +\delta\forall R.Cp(\alpha) \text{ then } \forall\beta \in \text{INDIV either}$$

(1) $-\delta R(\alpha, \beta)$ or
(2) $+\delta Cp(\beta)$

A proof for a positive defeasible role restriction $+\delta\forall R.Cp(\alpha)$ requires us to show that for every individual β in the domain, either R(α, β) cannot be proved or β belongs to the concept Cp. A proof for negative defeasible role restriction requires that we find an individual β such that R(α, β) can be defeasibly proved and that we cannot prove that β belongs to the concept Cp.

5 The Publication Ontology

Developing a publication ontology is not a straightforward process. Publications of an interdisciplinary nature can be looked at from different perspectives. After consulting librarians and various academics at the University of Jordan, we came to the conclusion that there is no single representation. For instance, different academic sections/departments in the same faculty may have different classifications of their books. A simple representation of the publication domain is shown in Fig. 1 below.

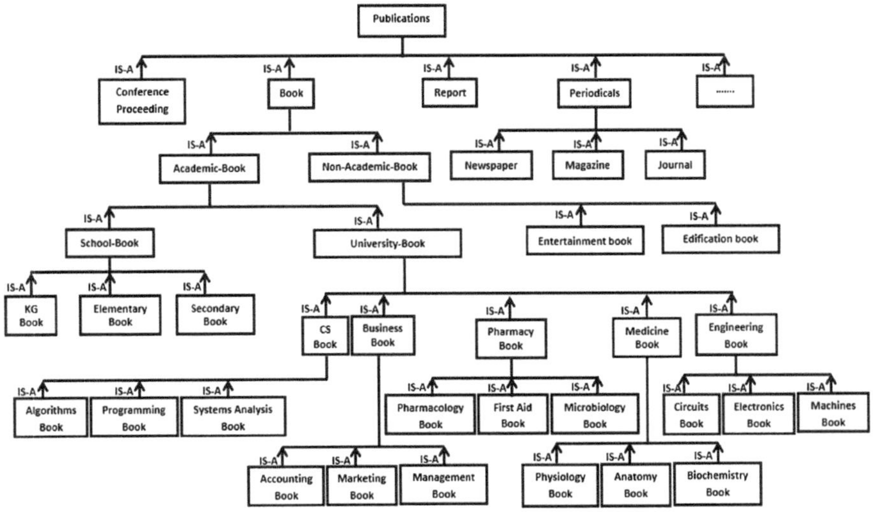

Fig. 1 Hierarchical structure of the publication domain

Before we introduce the rules, we shall use the following acronyms in brackets: Book (Bk), Publication (Pub), School-Book (Sch-Bk), Academic-Book (Acad-Bk), University-Book (Univ-Bk), Entertainment-Book (Ent-Bk), Non-Academic-Book (N-Acad-Bk), Edification-Book (Edi-Bk), KG-Book (KG-Bk), Elementary-Book (Elem-Bk), Secondary-Book (Sec-Bk), Used-for-Education (Used-Edu), Self-Study (S-Study), Business-Book (Bus-Bk), Pharmacy-Book (Phar-Bk), Medicine-Book (Med-Bk), Engineering-Book (Eng-Bk), Algorithms-Book (Alg-Bk), CS-Book (CS-Bk), Programming-Book (Prog-Bk), Systems-Analysis-Book (Sys-Ana-Bk), Accounting-Book (Acc-Bk), Marketing-Book (Mark-Bk), Management-Book (Manag-Bk), Pharmacology-Book (Pharco-Bk), FirstAid-Book (F-Aid-Bk), Microbiology-Book (Micro-Bk), Physiology-Book (Phys-Bk), Anatomy-Book (Anat-Bk), Biochemistry-Book (Bioch-Bk), Circuits-Book (Circ-Bk), Electronics-Book (Elect-Bk), Machines-Book (Mach-Bk), Engineering-Course (Eng-C), Business-Course (Bus-C), Medicine-Course (Med-C) and Pharmacy-Course (Phar-C).

Strict Rules

$$R_1 : Bk \rightarrow Pub \quad R_2 : Acad - Bk \rightarrow Bk \quad R_3 : N - Acad - Bk \rightarrow Bk$$

Defeasible Rules

$R_{4.1}$: Sch-Bk ⇒ Acad-Bk
$R_{4.2}$: Univ-Bk ⇒ Acad-Bk
$R_{5.1}$: Ent-Bk ⇒ N-Acad-Bk
$R_{5.2}$: Edi-Bk ⇒ N-Acad-Bk
$R_{6.1}$: KG-Bk ⇒ Sch-Bk
$R_{6.2}$: Elem-Bk ⇒ Sch-Bk
$R_{6.3}$: Sec-Bk ⇒ Sch-Bk
$R_{7.1}$: Univ-Bk ⇒ Acad-Bk
$R_{7.2}$: Univ-Bk,S-Study ⇒ N-Acad-Bk
$R_{8.1}$: Ent-Bk, Used-Edu ⇒ Acad-Bk
$R_{8.2}$: Edi-Bk, Used-Edu ⇒ Acad-Bk
$R_{9.1}$: CS-Bk ⇒ Univ-Bk
$R_{9.2}$: Bus-Bk ⇒ Univ-Bk
$R_{9.3}$: Phar-Bk ⇒ Univ-Bk
$R_{9.4}$: Med-Bk ⇒ Univ-Bk
$R_{9.5}$: Eng-Bk ⇒ Univ-Bk
$R_{10.1}$: Alg-Bk ⇒ CS-Bk
$R_{10.2}$: Prog-Bk ⇒ CS-Bk
$R_{10.3}$: Sys-Ana-Bk ⇒ CS-Bk
$R_{11.1}$: Acc-Bk ⇒ Bus-Bk
$R_{11.2}$: Mark-Bk ⇒ Bus-Bk
$R_{11.3}$: Manag-Bk ⇒ Bus-Bk
$R_{12.1}$: Pharco-Bk ⇒ Phar-Bk
$R_{12.2}$: F-Aid-Bk ⇒ Phar-Book
$R_{12.3}$: Micro-Bk ⇒ Phar-Bk
$R_{13.1}$: Phys-Bk ⇒ Med-Bk
$R_{13.2}$: Anat-Bk ⇒ Med-Bk
$R_{13.3}$: Bioch-Bk ⇒ Med-Bk
$R_{14.1}$: Circ-Bk ⇒ Eng-Bk
$R_{14.2}$: Elect-Bk ⇒ Eng-Bk
$R_{14.3}$: Mach-Bk ⇒ Eng-Bk
R_{15}: Prog-Bk, Eng-C ⇒ Eng-Bk
R_{16}: Sys-Ana-Bk,Bus-C ⇒ Bus-Bk
R_{17}: Micro-Bk, Med-C ⇒ Med-Bk
R_{18}: Anat-Bk, Phar-C ⇒ Phar-Bk

To help the reader in following the rules we take $R_{5,1}$ which states that a typical entertainment book is a nonacademic book. A close look shows that some of the rules are contradictory. For instance, the following pairs: ($R_{5.1}$, $R_{8.1}$), ($R_{5.2}$, $R_{8.2}$), ($R_{10,2}$, R_{15}), ($R_{12,3}$, R_{17}), and ($R_{10,2}$, R_{15}) are contradictory. A superiority relation between contradictory rules could resolve inconsistency when these rules are applicable and give the desired conclusions in the proper situation. For instance, using (S_1) $R_{8.1} > R_{5.1}$ resolves the conflict and allow us to conclude that *Romeo and Juliet* is an academic book. Using (S_2) $R_{8.2} > R_{5.2}$ allows us to conclude that the book entitled *Children's Book of Virtues* published in the year 1995, which is an edification book and used for education in schools, is an academic book. Similarly, using (S_3) $R_{15} > R_{10,2}$ allows us to conclude that the book entitled *Introduction to C++ Programming*, which is typically a programming book and used by engineering students is an engineering book. In the same way we could employ (S_4) $R_{16} > R_{10,3}$ and (S_5) $R_{17} > R_{12,3.}$

What is clear from the discussion above is that the superiority relation gives us a ranking of the rules which could be adjusted to meet the needs of users. That is, we need a dynamic ranking which results in dynamic classifications as needed.

6 Relevant Literature

There are many approaches that have been suggested to add nonmonotonicity to description logic systems. The most relevant to our work is the approach presented in [19]. It proposes to add defeasible rules to ontologies captured in description logic. In the language which they employ, they distinguish between normal literals and description logic literals. The description logic literals occur only in the antecedent of the defeasible rules, whereas the normal literals could occur in both the antecedents and the consequents of the defeasible rules and thus they show a nonmonotonic behavior. The approach, in [20], made an attempt to improve the expressive power of description logic by studying programs expressed in description logic and description horn logic. An attempt is made in [21] to extend the description logic system *SHOQ* by adding a preference relation between rules that parallels the superiority relation which we used in *DefL*.

Some of the relevant implemented projects include the JeromeDL project [22] which employs Semantic Web technologies mainly for user management and personalized search within a digital library. It does not perform any kind of knowledge extraction. The SIMILE Project [23] made an attempt to enhance interoperability among digital assets, vocabularies, metadata, and services. The FEDORA project [24] aimed to support the whole digital content value chain from data creation, sharing, search and dynamic provision of appropriate services.

7 Conclusions

We have made a first step toward developing defeasible description logic that can represent a flexible publication ontology which can support intelligent queries. We have employed the description logic system *ALC* to build the ontology. We have investigated extending an *ALC* knowledge base with defeasible rules in order to develop a flexible and decidable reasoning system called *Def-ALC* that can be of benefit to users of a digital library. It is important to note that neither description logic nor defeasible logic is suitable for reasoning with incomplete information in a decidable manner. Therefore, an attempt to properly integrate both systems is beneficial. *ALC* is a decidable fragment of FOPC. Therefore, it assumes complete knowledge and it cannot deal with inconsistency. Defeasible logic allows us to reason with knowledge bases when conflicting information is present.

We have developed and implemented a prototype of a publication ontology *Def-ALC*. The work is far from complete. A more through study of, and comparison with, other systems that employ a knowledge base implemented using description logic is needed.

References

1. Arms WY (2001) Digital libraries. The MIT Press, Cambridge
2. Garcia-Castro A, Labarga A, Garcia L, Giraldo O, Montaña C, Bateman JA (2010) Semantic web and social web heading towards living documents in the life sciences. web semantics: science, services and agents on the World Wide Web, vol 8, pp 155–162
3. Shotton D, Portwin K, Klyne G, Miles A (2009) Adventures in semantic publishing: exemplar semantic enhancement of a research article. PLoS Comput Biol 5(4):e100036124
4. Baader F, McGuiness D, Nardi D, Patel-Schneider P (2003) The description logic handbook: theory, implementation and applications. Cambridge University Press, Cambridge
5. Moubaiddin A, Obeid N (2008) Dialogue and argumentation in multi-agent diagnosis. In: New challenges in applied intelligence technologies, studies in computational intelligence, vol 134. Springer, Heidelberg, pp 13–22
6. Moubaiddin A, Obeid N (2009) Partial information basis for agent-based collaborative dialogue. Appl Intell 30(2):142–167
7. Moubaiddin A, Obeid N (2007) The role of dialogue in remote diagnostics. In: Proceedings of 20th international conference on condition monitoring and diagnostic engineering management, pp 677–686
8. Moubaiddin A, Obeid N (2013) On formalizing social commitments in dialogue and argumentation models using temporal defeasible logic. Knowl Inf Syst 37(2):417–452
9. Nute D (1994) Defeasible logic In: Handbook of logic in artificial intelligence and logic programming, vol 3. Oxford University Press, Oxford, pp 353–395
10. Obeid N (1996) Three valued logic and nonmonotonic reasoning. Comput Artif Intell 15(6): 509–530
11. Obeid N (2000) Towards a model of learning through communication. Knowl Inf Syst 2(4): 498–508
12. Obeid N (2005) A Formalism for Representing and Reasoning with Temporal Information event and change. Appl Intell 23(2):109–119
13. Obeid N, Moubaiddin A (2009) On the role of dialogue and argumentation in collaborative problem solving. In: Proceedings of 9th international conference on intelligent systems design and applications. IEEE, pp 1202–1208
14. Obeid N, Rao RB (2010) On integrating event definition and event detection. Knowl Inf Syst 22(2):129–158
15. Sabri KE, Obeid N (2016) A temporal defeasible logic for handling access control policies. Appl Intell 44(1):30–42
16. Governatori G, Maher M, Antoniou G, Billington D (2004) Argumentation semantics for defeasible logic. J Logic Comput 14(5):675–702
17. Governatori G (2005) Representing business contracts in RuleML. Int J Cooper Inf Syst 14(2–3):181–216
18. Guarino N (1998) Formal ontology in information systems. In: Proceedings of FOIS'98, pp 3–15
19. Wang K, Billington D, Blee J, Antoniou G (2004) Combining description logic and defeasible logic for the semantic web. LNCS, Springer, Heidelberg
20. Grosof I, Horrocks R, Volz S, Decker S (2003) Description logic programs: combining logic programs with description logic. In: 12th International conference on World Wide. ACM Press, pp 48–57
21. Grigoris A, Wagner G (2003) Rules and defeasible reasoning on the semantic web. In: Schroeder M, Wagner G (eds) RuleML 2003. LNCS, vol 2876. Springer, Berlin, pp 111–120

22. Kruk SR, Decker S, Zieborak L (2005) Jeromedl adding semantic web technologies to digital libraries. Lecture notes in computer science, vol 3588. Springer, Heidelberg, pp 716–725
23. Mazzocchi S, Garland S, Lee R (2006) Simile: practical metadata for the semantic Web. XML.com
24. Payette S, Staples T (2002) The mellon fedora project: digital library architecture meets XML and Web services. LNCS, vol 2459. Springer, Heidelberg, pp 406–421

Exploiting Social Media and Tagging for Social Book Search: Simple Query Methods for Retrieval Optimization

Faten Hamad and Bashar Al-Shboul

Abstract With web and social media information availability and accessibility increasing on the one hand, there is an increased complexity of retrieval on the other. Generally, real information needs are complex to express. Books are the prevailing information resources and book searching is one of the online activities that users attempt daily. Mobile technology makes it easy to handle books, i.e., ibook and kindle formats; however, locating users' preference over the Internet is still quite complex. Efforts are being made to help users locate their desired books easily and quickly. This research is set up to investigate techniques to support users in searching and navigating the full texts of digitized books and complementary social media in order to enhance the user book search experience. The idea is based on the INEX SBS track to use professional metadata and user-generated metadata to enhance the retrieval process of books by optimizing simple search query with INEX SBS 2015. Amazon and LibraryThing book descriptions were processed to extract information and important fields to be indexed. The proposed model use the Named Entity Recognition tagger (NER) and the Part-Of-Speech tagger (POS) to extract relevant topics that are related to book search. The results indicated that using simple methods such as NER and POS tagging can generate an effective query for book retrieval.

Keywords Social book search · INEX · User-generated metadata · Social tagging · Social media · E-publishing

F. Hamad (✉)
Department of Library and Information Science, School of Educational Sciences, The University of Jordan, Amman, Jordan
e-mail: f.hamad@ju.edu.jo

B. Al-Shboul (✉)
Department of Business Information Technology, King Abdullah II School for Information Technology, The University of Jordan, Amman, Jordan
e-mail: bashar.shboul@gmail.com

N. Taha et al. (eds.), *Social Media Shaping e-Publishing and Academia*,
DOI 10.1007/978-3-319-55354-2_9

1 Introduction

Finding information and information resources is challenging due to the complexity of retrieval system required to recognize human information needs precisely, especially with the growing numbers of online portals and book catalogues. Books are considered the dominant information resource, and accordingly efforts are being made to help users locate the required book(s). The new era of information retrieval has introduced new search types with useful features by creating networks of entities. Recently, social tagging, social searches and personalized searches have become wide spread. Users create their own tags that reflect their interests and presences [1]. User-generated content to annotate web resources is playing a greater role in improving Information Retrieval (IR) tasks. They can contribute to enhancing the retrieval process by acting as meaningful keywords bridging the gap between humans and machines [1].

Amazon is one of the pioneer online book sellers; it is well known to have a robust e-publishing system. Amazon allows users to search for books in their interface and provides users with other users' feedback and reviews about books [2]. It is highly focused on gaining buyer reviews and ratings and then promotes the use of reviews throughout the visitor's experience before and after the purchase. Amazon provides recommendations based on users' social profile and activities and uses data from other users' behaviors and search history. Social media and reviews are considered part of the marketing lifecycle and book promotion. Customer reviews, ratings, and social comments are used to help site editors get a sense of how readers are responding to a book, and then use this to choose which books to promote. It helps other users to search for books they have interests in. Moreover, Amazon supports mobile book searching via kindle versions of books, so it becomes easier to search for books using your mobile device. This easy interaction needs support from the system to help users locate their preferences easily and quickly. In addition, it has Amazon Web Services (AWS) as a secure cloud services platform to offer customers computing power, database storage, content delivery, and other functionality to help businesses scale and grow. Accordingly, the business of e-publishing is continuously growing being supported by Amazon's continuous support and improvements to its services. In line with this, book search becomes easier but complex at the same time. So all the user needs to do is to locate what they need and enjoy the benefits from these types of services and technology.

LibraryThing uses Amazon and libraries that provide open access to their collections with the Z39.50 protocol. The protocol is used by a variety of desktop programmes, notably bibliographic software like EndNote [3]. It provides blog to discuss books, so users can exchange experience about books they have read or are about to read.

Social book search is a complex retrieval system to understand; therefore, achieving optimal retrieval is not straightforward [4]. The Social Book Search Track was launched by INEX in 2007 with the purpose of providing support to users in terms of easy search and access to books using metadata and fully digitized books [5].

INEX provides a relevant experimental platform to investigate techniques for searching and navigating professional metadata as well as for user-generated content from social media. This chapter investigates techniques to support users in searching and navigating the full texts of books in digital form and complementary social media in order to enhance the user book search experience.

This chapter is organized as follows. In the first section, a review of the existing literature on the subject is introduced. Section 2 discusses the methodology of this research. The experimental setup is discussed in Sect. 3. Evaluation and results analysis is presented in Sect. 4. And finally, the conclusion of this research is presented in Sect. 5.

2 Literature Review

Social searching and social tagging (user-generated content) are receiving more attention than ever before, especially with the growth of social networking tools and the wealth of information available on the web. Many researchers recommend incorporating social tagging into the library environment. For instance, Lee et al. [1] proposed a social inverted index—an extended inverted index for social tagging-based information retrieval. The social inverted index maintains a separate user-generated sublist for each resource in a resource posting list to contain each user's features as weights. Lee et al. findings indicated that social inverted indexing performs better in IR tasks than a normal inverted index. One interesting aspect of user-generated metadata appears to be the smaller gap with the vocabulary of searchers [4]. In line with this, Zhang et al. [6] found that index that is enriched with user-generated data improves the retrieval effectiveness, and tags are the best-performed social feature on re-ranking.

Lu et al. [7] compared user-generated social tags from the LibraryThing website with the subject terms assigned by professionals at the Library of Congress Subject Headings (LCSH), to examine the difference between social tags and expert-assigned subject terms. Their findings showed that using social tags in library systems is possible and can improve the accessibility of library collections. They recommended that library cataloguing systems should change their traditional ways of cataloguing to incorporate subject-related tags within the library system.

The INitiative for the Evaluation of XML Retrieval (INEX) was started in 2001 as a forum aiming to improve the retrieval of relevant elements. It provides a platform for organizations to compete on XML-based retrieval tasks and compare the results [8]. Social Book Search (SBS) was introduced by INEX in 2007 in an attempt to support users in searching, navigating, and reading book metadata and the full text of books in digitized form [5]. The idea is combining both professional metadata and user-generated content (social media content) to enhance the retrieval task and to meet users' information needs.

Social book search literature appears to be limited as the background of this research span over the period between 2011 until 2015. In INEX 2011, for example, the document collection consists of 211 topics and 2.8 million book descriptions from Amazon and LibraryThing. The track aims at studying the relative value of user-generated metadata compared to controlled metadata. The track involved generation of a ranked list of books to determine the effect of professional and social metadata (i.e., tags, reviews, and user-generated content from LibraryThing and Amazon) on the results [5]. In INEX 2012, the focus changed from the relative value of professional and user-generated metadata to the complexity of book search information needs [9]. The number of topics increased to 300 topics where the document collection contains more description of books from the Library of Congress and the British Library. The nature of book requests and suggestions from users' profiles (LibraryThing forum) are considered to be information needs statements and relevance judgments, and therefore, user's cognition and preference was used as part of the retrieval process to see if there were improvements over the traditional system [9].

The INEX 2013 task delved deeper into the nature of book research information needs and book suggestions from the LibraryThing forums [10]. In INEX 2014, the task remained as the last year's evaluation. It found that most SBS requirements are mainly related to books' contents (i.e., topic, genre, familiarity, and engagement) and are important aspects for retrieval [11]. The INEX 2015 topic format is an extension of the 2014 topics. For instance, all the fields in the 2014 topics are present; in addition, there is an example field which lists all the example books mentioned in the book search request [12].

Social book search is a complex retrieval system to understand and optimize. In this context, Koolen et al. [4] used INEX 2011 Books and Social Search Track's collection of book descriptions from Amazon and the LibraryThing social cataloguing site to compare classical IR with social book search. Koolen et al. stressed that user-generated content is more effective for social book search than professional metadata. Ravva et al. [13] presented a designed recommender system that uses similar users as its basis for grouping books. This method uses both user-generated and professional metadata, which is similar to our work that followed the 'suggestion' track which suggested a ranked list of books to satisfy the user's query.

In line with this, Koolen et al. [14] studied complex information requests in social media with a focus on social book search. They based their research on a large set of annotated book requests from the LibraryThing discussion forums to analyse. The results indicated that book search requests combine the search and recommendation aspects in a complicated way which requires that traditional systems improve their search approaches to handle such complex search requests. Koolen et al. results showed retrieval systems can use the content aspects of the search requests, while recommender systems pick up signals in the requester's catalogue such as content, context, and example. Furthermore, Kumar and Pal [15] confirmed that it is imperative to use both user profiles and user catalogues. Wu et al. [16] integrate social features into the retrieval system in order to provide a better recommendation on books. They argued that recommendations from experienced users may contain things and aspects that traditional systems are not able to capture. It reflects the level of knowledge of users [17, 18].

3 Methodology

This research is based on two phases: the indexing and the retrieval phases as shown in Fig. 1. The main framework in the first phase is the data extraction which includes the books and related information about them. In this experiment the Lemur Project/Indri tool was utilized to obtain the important fields to be indexed. Lemur is a collection of software tools and search engines, designed to support research on using statistical language models for information retrieval tasks [19]. Indri is a search index that comes with Lemur [20]. It can handle large collections of data and can understand various data formats like HTML and XML [20]. In other words, the relevant topics which are related to our basic book search are extracted.

In this experiment, the data used in the indexing process is book description documents from Amazon/LibraryThing (A/LT). The document collection consists of descriptions with metadata for approximately 2.8 million books [8]. The data used in the retrieval process is 2014 topic's sets each of which contains information about a certain topic. The narrative tag has the description of the information need and one or more example books provided by the topic creator. Figure 2 shows a sample of a topic set.

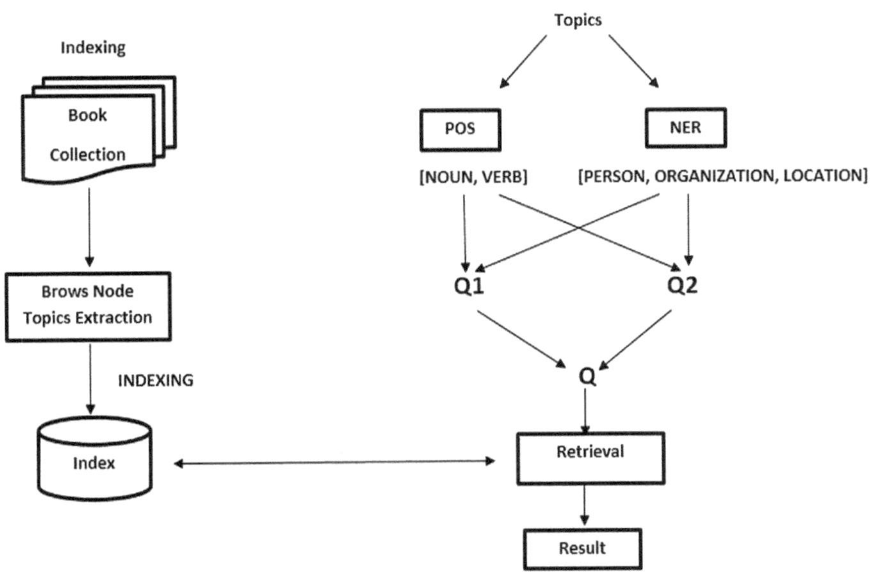

Fig. 1 Indexing and the retrieval process

```
- <topic id="74">
    <title>Los Angeles Loves Librarything Message Board</title>
    <group>Los Angeles Loves Librarything</group>
    <narrative>I don't actually live in LA yet, but I'm moving there - from London - on Tuesday.
        Any book recommendations for preparing myself through the medium of fiction?
        </narrative>
  - <types>
        <type>subject</type>
    </types>
  - <genres>
        <genre>literature - prose</genre>
    </genres>
    <specificity>broad</specificity>
    <similar/>
    <dissimilar/>
  </topic>
```


Fig. 2 Topic set document

The descriptions from Amazon.com are enriched with user-generated content from LibraryThing. Furthermore, each book description contains publishers' supplied metadata (i.e., book title, author, publisher, year of publication); subject metadata (i.e., classification code, subject headings); and user-generated content (i.e., Amazon user ratings, reviews, and LibraryThing user tags). Figure 3 illustrates book description.

Next, important tags were extracted using the two Stanford's taggers, in order to form queries to improve the search process for the required books. First, the Named Entity Recognition (NER) tagger was employed [21]. It labels sequences of words in a text which are the names of things, i.e., persons and company names. Using NER, three main entities, which are [PERSON, ORGANIZATION AND LOCATION], were extracted and chosen; those which appeared to be the most used entities by users for searching for books were author name and publisher name. Second, the Part-Of-Speech tagger (POS) was adopted. It reads text and assigns parts of speech to each word (and other tokens), such as noun, verb, adjective, etc. [22]. Using POS [VERBS, NOUNS, and ADJECTIVES] were extracted as they appeared frequently in the searching process and were very common in book titles and descriptions.

After the tagging process was completed, queries for searching and retrieval were formed to search in the index output. This results in obtaining book recommendations; see Fig. 4.

The first query used the #combine operator to combine the outputs of the two taggers together [VERBS, NOUNS, ADJECTIVES, PERSON, LOCATION, ORGANIZATION] into a single query.

- #combine($T_1, \ldots, T_n$).

This operator combines the query terms (T_i), which will result in finding a ranked list of books which match specified queries; see Fig. 5.

The second query was more complex. It was formed by assigning 0.4 weight to VERBS, NOUNS, and ADJECTIVES and assigning 0.6 weight to the named entities [PERSON, LOCATION, ORGANIZATION] using #weight; see Fig. 5.

- #weight($w_1 T_1, \ldots, w_n T_n$).

```
<book>
        <isbn>000219709X</isbn>
<title>The Wild Flowers of Britain and Northern Ireland (Collins
Handguides) </title>
[
<subject>Revolution,1775-1783</subject>
<source>Product Description</source>

<name>RosemaryWise</name>
<role>Author</role>

<similarproduct>0226874001</similarproduct>

        <browseNodes>
<browseNode id="1000">Subjects</browseNode>
<browseNode id="173507">Professional &amp;
Technical</browseNode>
<browseNode id="173510">Professional Science</browseNode>
<browseNode id="227254">Agricultural Sciences</browseNode>
<browseNode id="227430">Forestry</browseNode>
<browseNode id="283155">Books</browseNode>
<browseNode id="388186011">Refinements</browseNode>
<browseNode id="394174011">Binding (binding)</browseNode>
<browseNode id="400272011">Paperback</browseNode>
<browseNode id="618072011">Format (feature_browse-bin)
</browseNode>
<browseNode id="618083011">Printed Books</browseNode>
<browseNode id="713580011">General AAS</browseNode>
        </browseNodes>
</book>

- <reviews>
  - <review>
      <authorid>A16IWS0FHK6YUQ</authorid>
      <date>2008-11-09</date>
      <summary>Personal Growth</summary>
      <content>This is a good book if you really want to know how to feel closer to Christ. It might be hard at first
        but like all things, if you are diligent, you will see wonderful results. It also has very beautiful pictures
        from Simon Dewey. You will not regret buying this book for yourself or a good friend in need.</content>
      <rating>5</rating>
      <totalvotes>1</totalvotes>
      <helpfulvotes>1</helpfulvotes>
    </review>
  - <review>
      <authorid>AUZP1P5854TF2</authorid>
      <date>2008-12-22</date>
      <summary>beautiful and useful</summary>
      <content>this book is absolutely gorgeous and enjoyable. each chapter concerns a different part about
        Christ's life, and includes a couple of pages about the topic as well as scripture references to read,
        things to ponder. I think it will work perfectly for a chapter a week at family home evening, in personal
        study, and for devotionals. also just a great table book! </content>
      <rating>5</rating>
      <totalvotes>1</totalvotes>
      <helpfulvotes>1</helpfulvotes>
    </review>
  </reviews>
- <editorialreviews>
  - <editorialreview>
      <source>Product Description</source>
      <content>Nestled between the covers of this beautifully illustrated book is an invitation--an invitation to
        come closer to Christ through a 21-day journey. Each step of the journey introduces a new concept that
        will help you come to know and recognize the hand of the Lord in your life. With an emphasis on daily
        scripture study and personal prayer, each chapter concludes with an assignement designed to help you
        apply and personalize concepts such as humility, gratitude, and listening to the Spirit. In the rush of
        everyday life, this unique book provides a refreshing pause and the opportunity to focus our efforts on
        becoming closer to Christ.</content>
    </editorialreview>
  </editorialreviews>
```


Fig. 3 Book description document

Weights decide the impact a word has on the query; the higher the weight, the higher the relevance and impact.

Queries were combined with linear interpolation as follows:

$$Q = \alpha_1 Q_1 + \alpha_2 Q_2 \tag{1}$$

where $\alpha_1 + \alpha_2 = 1$.

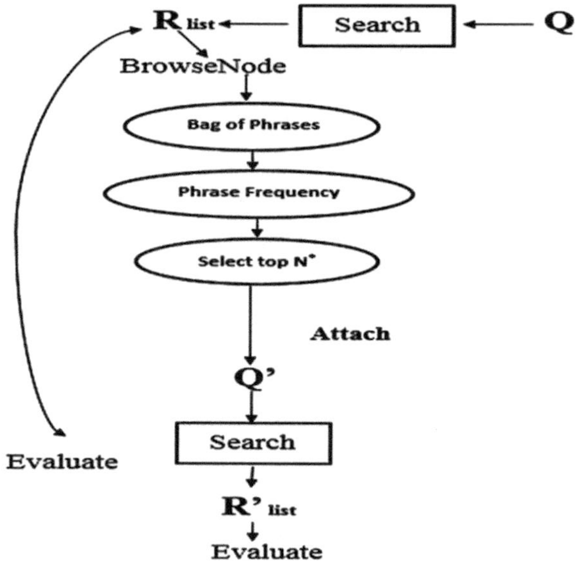

Fig. 4 Query construction process

Query 1 Sample

1196 : #combine(knew volunteer margarita people lead try chingiz novels learn central concept reasons hundred bulgakov surreality norm do world post peace thought looking concerns made novel preconceptions give years remnants lasts country is work read volunteers master was sanity be part reading start life let day makes crumbling vapor typifies head survived concrete anything have had service knew volunteer margarita people lead try chingiz novels learn central concept reasons hundred bulgakov surreality norm do world post peace thought looking concerns made novel preconceptions give years remnants lasts country is work read volunteers master was sanity be part reading start life let day makes crumbling vapor typifies head survived concrete anything have had readers service knew volunteer margarita people lead try chingiz novels learn central concept reasons hundred bulgakov surreality norm do corps world post peace thought looking concerns made novel preconceptions give years remnants lasts country is work read volunteers master was sanity be part reading start life let day makes crumbling vapor typifies head survived concrete anything have had readers service Soviet Best Novel Bulgakov Asia Volunteer Central Returned Readers Chingiz Corps Margarita Peace Aitmitov)
1584 : #combine(rice salt histories robinson ones recommendations robert kim years fatherland enjoyed rice salt histories robinson travel ones recommendations robert kim years fatherland worlds enjoyed rice salt history histories robinson travel ones recommendations robert books kim years fatherland worlds enjoyed Kim Robinson Time Harris Stanley Travel John Parallel Robert Worlds)

Query 2 Sample

1196 : #weight (0.4 #combine(knew volunteer margarita people lead try chingiz novels learn central concept reasons hundred bulgakov surreality norm do world post peace thought looking concerns made novel preconceptions give years remnants lasts country is work read volunteers master was sanity be part reading start life let day makes crumbling vapor typifies head survived concrete anything have had service knew volunteer margarita people lead try chingiz novels learn central concept reasons hundred bulgakov surreality norm do world post peace thought looking concerns made novel preconceptions give years remnants lasts country is work read volunteers master was sanity be part reading start life let day makes crumbling vapor typifies head survived concrete anything have had readers service knew volunteer margarita people lead try chingiz novels learn central concept reasons hundred bulgakov surreality norm do corps world post peace thought looking concerns made novel preconceptions give years remnants lasts country is work read volunteers master was sanity be part reading start life let day makes crumbling vapor typifies head survived concrete anything have had readers service) 0.6 #combine(Soviet Best Novel Bulgakov Asia Volunteer Central Returned Readers Chingiz Corps Margarita Peace Aitmitov))
1584 : #weight (0.4 #combine(rice salt histories robinson ones recommendations robert kim years fatherland enjoyed rice salt histories robinson travel ones recommendations robert kim years fatherland worlds enjoyed rice salt history histories robinson travel ones recommendations robert books kim years fatherland worlds enjoyed) 0.6 #combine(Kim Robinson Time Harris Stanley Travel John Parallel Robert Worlds))

Fig. 5 Queries sample

Weights 0.4 and 0.6 for α_1 and α_2 appeared to be the best combination after several trials of weights. Mean average precision (MAP) was used to measure retrieval performance, [23, 24]:

$$\text{MAPi} = \frac{1}{|R_i|}\sum\nolimits_{k=1}^{|R_i|} P(R_i[k]) \tag{2}$$

where R_i = total number of relevant records to the query q_i
$R_i[k]$ = the k-th document in R_i.

Table 1 Retrieval performance evaluation results compared to previous year's results

	# of topics	MAP	Rank	No. of teams
2014	680	0.3801	22	40
2015	208	0.2645	1	47

Finally, after completing the queries, the TREC_EVAL tool was used for the evaluation process, given the results file and a standard set of judged results [25].

In general, information retrieval systems compute a numeric score on how well each book in the index matches the query and ranks the books in a descending order according to this score. Okapi BM25 function was used to compute the matching score.

4 Evaluation and Results Analysis

Mean average precision (MAP) for years 2014 and 2015 was calculated. Table 1 shows a comparison between this research study's results and 2014 suggestions results. It illustrated that results and ranking of the proposed simple query methods is better than the 2014 year's results. In terms of mean average precision (MAP), our experiment reported a MAP of 0.2645, compared to reported results of the 2014 MAP of 0.3801. Compared to year 2015, it is reported that our MAP score is ranked first.

It appears the proposed simple query search methods can enhance the social book searching process. Social user-generated content (social media content) such as reviews and rating seems to improve the searching process and experience of the users.

5 Conclusion

The main goal of this study is to develop a retrieval method that can meet users' requests and handle the diversity of them. This research used both professional metadata and user-generated content (social media content) to enhance book searching and retrieval using book description from Amazon—a big e-book e-publisher and seller—and LibraryThing. The results indicated that the use of some simple methods like Named Entity Recognizer (NER) tagging and Part-Of-Speech (POS) tagging in addition to some operators such as #combine and #weight can generate a very effective query compared to other runs and other experiments' results, which might result in an improved retrieval performance.

In future work the methods to form new queries might be changed in order to get different results, such as modifying the weights or changing the language model. Other semantically related methods (or structured corpora) should be explored further to see how much more the retrieval result might be changed or enhanced.

References

1. Lee Kim HG, Kim HJ (2012) A social inverted index for social-tagging-based information retrieval. J Inf Sci 38(4):313–332. doi:10.1177/0165551512438357
2. Amazon. http://www.amazon.com. Accessed 29 Feb 2016
3. LibraryThing. https://www.librarything.com/about. Accessed 29 Feb 2016
4. Koolen M, Kamps J, Kazai G (2012) Social book search: comparing topical relevance judgements and book suggestions for evaluation. In: Proceedings of the 21st ACM international conference on information and knowledge management (CIKM'12). ACM. New York, USA, pp 185–194. doi:http://dx.doi.org/10.1145/2396761.2396788
5. Koolen M, Kazai G, Kamps J, Doucet A and Landoni M (2011) Overview of the INEX 2011 books and social search track. In: Focused retrieval of content and structure 2011, Dec 12, Springer, Heidelberg, pp 1–29
6. Zhang BW, Yin XC, Cui XP, Qu J, Geng B, Zhou F, Hao HW (2014) USTB at INEX2014: social book search track. In: Fourth international conference of the cross-language evaluation forum (CLEF, working notes), pp 536–542
7. Lu C, Jung-ran P, Hu X (2010) User tags versus expert-assigned subject terms: a comparison of librarything tags and library of congress subject headings. J Inf Sci 36(6):763–779
8. INEX: About INEX. http://inex.mmci.uni-saarland.de/about.html. (2014, Accessed 15 July 2015)
9. Koolen M, Kazai G, Kamps J, Preminger M, Doucet A, Landoni M (2015) Overview of the INEX 2012 social book search track. http://e.humanities.uva.nl/publications/2012/kool:over12b.pdf. Accessed 15 July 2015
10. Koolen M, Kazai G, Preminger M, Doucet A (2013) Overview of the INEX 2013 social book search track. In: Information access evaluation meets multilinguality, multimodality, and visualization-fourth international conference of the cross-language evaluation forum, CLEF 2013, p 26
11. Bogers T, Koolen M, Kamps J et al (2014) Overview of the INEX 2014 social book search track. In: Conference and labs of the evaluation forum, pp 462–479
12. Koolen M, Bogers T, Kamps J (2015) Overview of the INEX 2015 social book search suggestion track. Online reference. In: Conference and labs of the evaluation forum. http://social-book-search.humanities.uva.nl/#/publications. Accessed 16 July 2015
13. Ravva V, Singampalli LL, Krishna V, Thotempudi VK, Crouch CJ (Date required) A methodology for social book search
14. Koolen M, Bogers T, van den Bosch A et al (2015) Looking for books in social media: an analysis of complex search requests. In: 37th European conference on IR research, ECIR 2015, 29 March – 2 April, Vienna, Austria, pp 184–196
15. Kumar R, Pal S (2014) Social book search track: ISM@ INEX'14 suggestion task. In: Fourth international conference of the cross-language evaluation forum (CLEF, working notes), pp 521–524
16. Wu SH, Liao PK, Lin HW, Hsu LJ, Xiao WL, Chen LP and Chen GD (2014) Query type recognition and result filtering in INEX 2014 social book search track. In: Fourth international conference of the cross-language evaluation forum (CLEF, working notes), pp 525–535
17. Thotempudi VK (2014) A recommender system for social book search. Ph.D. thesis, University of Minnesota, USA

18. Singampalli LL (2014) Social book search: a methodology that combines both retrieval and recommendation. Ph.D. thesis, University of Minnesota, USA
19. Lemur. http://www.lemurproject.org/about.php. Accessed 27 July 2015
20. Lemur. http://www.lemurproject.org/indri/. Accessed 27 July 2015
21. The stanford natural language processing group. Stanford named entity recognizer (NER). http://nlp.stanford.edu/software/CRF-NER.shtm. Accessed 25 July 2015
22. The stanford natural language processing group. Stanford log-linear part-of-speech tagger. http://nlp.stanford.edu/software/tagger.shtml. Accessed 25 July 2015
23. Zuva K and Zuva T (2012) Evaluation of information retrieval systems. Int J Comput Sci Inf Technol IJCSIT 4(3)
24. Baeza-Yatez R, Robeiro-Neto B (2011) Modern information retrieval, 2nd edn. Addison Wesely Longman, Essex, pp 135–141
25. Trec-Eval. http://trec.nist.gov/trec_eval/. Accessed 25 July 2015

Part IV
Security and Privacy in the Era of Social Media

In the context of OSNs, users post and share a range of multimedia content such text, links, pictures, and videos. This makes these platforms an extremely interactive virtual environment in which huge amounts of personal and private information is stored and exchanged. On the other hand, the availability of such personal information attracts cybercriminals whose malicious activities have become easier with the increased popularity of OSNs. Many security attacks became more prevalent and much more dangerous due to the nature of OSNs. For instance, online social phishing attack by which the user is tricked into sharing sensitive information is more likely to succeed compared to random email phishing.

This increase in the flow of electronic information over OSNs raises many concerns about the secure storage, processing, and exchange of personal information. Consequently, the term 'information security' has evolved to include several issues with a strong social foundation such as trust, privacy, legal liability, and intellectual property rights. Additionally, several parties became involved and have interest in this domain; these include governments, citizens/customers, and businesses together with technology vendors and academic researchers.

To cover the various security issues in the context of OSNs this part provides a chapter that examines online social networks security and looks at threats, attacks and future directions. The aim of this chapter is to discuss how serious security attacks are possible in OSNs and what has been done to counter them. It will discuss privacy, Sybil attacks, social engineering, spam, malware, botnet attacks, and the trade-off between services, security and users' rights. The authors of this chapter argue that there is a need for suggesting models and technical solutions to counter the emerging security threats. Finally, the chapter presents a set of possible future research directions based on the identified security attacks.

Ja'far Alqatawna

Online Social Networks Security: Threats, Attacks, and Future Directions

Ja'far Alqatawna, Alia Madain, Ala' M. Al-Zoubi and Rizik Al-Sayyed

Abstract A list of well-known Online Social Networks extend to hundreds of available sites with hundreds of thousands, millions, and even billions of registered accounts; for instance, Facebook as of April 2016 has around two billion active users. Online Social Networks made a difference in many people's lives and helped in opening avenues that were not possible before. However, as in any success story there is a downside. Cyber-attacks that used to have a small or limited effect can now have a huge distributed effect through utilizing those social network sites. Some attacks are more apparent than others in this context; hence this chapter discusses how serious attacks are possible in online social networks and what has been done to encounter them. It will discuss privacy, Sybil attacks, social engineering, spam, malware, botnet attacks, and the trade-off between services, security, and users' rights.

1 Introduction

Online Social Networks (OSNs) brought much of the positive change in our world today. Nevertheless, there is a dark side of all of this development. OSNs impact individuals, groups, and countries. Moreover, they could be used as a base to cause damage in both the real world and the virtual world [27].

Security and privacy in OSNs is a hot topic for investigation today, since its outcomes are critical and affect many lives. Although there are no inherent fundamental threats in OSNs, taking into consideration the range of applications to

J. Alqatawna (✉) · A. Madain · A.M. Al-Zoubi · R. Al-Sayyed
King Abdulla II School for Information Technology, University of Jordan, Amman, Jordan
e-mail: j.alqatawna@ju.edu.jo

J. Alqatawna
Jordan Information Security & Digital Forensics Research Group (JISDF), Amman, Jordan

N. Taha et al. (eds.), *Social Media Shaping e-Publishing and Academia*,
DOI 10.1007/978-3-319-55354-2_10

which OSNs may be applied makes the network an enabler of existing well-known security and privacy exploits [47]. For example, OSNs can cause threats to the privacy and security of health information, when combined with applications in health care [48].

Many believe that the privacy settings offered by social networks gives just the psychological feeling of being private. It is just an illusion, since nothing online can be considered completely private and once the information is online, it is recorded for a long time if not forever. In the case of social networks, the problem of keeping private information private becomes much more complicated with multiple factors coming into play.

Research in the area of OSN security and privacy can be categorized in multiple ways. For instance, the type of network and technology used in the OSN can be the base of security issues classification since some issues are more apparent in one technology than in another and some solutions are applicable to a certain type of technology and/or architecture. Bodriagov and Buchegger [15], Graffi et al. [28], and Jahid et al. [32] focus on Peer-to-Peer (P2P) social networks, while Beach et al. [10] focus on mobile social networking.

Additionally, research in this area can be categorized based on the countermeasure it provides and when it is applied. The countermeasure can be used to prevent, limit, predict, or recover from attacks. Another possible categorization is based on the attacker; for example, when privacy is the focus of the research, breaches can come from the social network site itself, third-party applications, other users, [26] or even governments.

The categorization we use here is based on the attack, and unlike Cutillo et al. [21], we focus on a minimal number of attacks relevant to the context of OSNs; the attacks are chosen based on how OSNs made these well-known attacks more exploitable and more dangerous. Cutillo et al. [21] discuss potential attacks in the context of OSNs as follows: identity theft, profile cloning, profile porting, secondary data collection, profiling, communication tracking, face recognition, image retrieval, harvesting, fake profiles, Sybil attacks, ballot stuffing, defamation, censorship, and finally collusion.

In this chapter, we try to simplify things and focus on recent advancements in attacking and protecting OSNs and discuss the trade-off between services, security, and stakeholders' rights. The rest of the chapter is organized as follows: Sect. 2 presents a thorough discussion on privacy related issues; Sect. 3 covers Sybil attacks; Sect. 4 presents some of the work done in social engineering attacks; Sect. 5 covers spam; Sect. 6 discusses how OSNs can become a platform for malware and botnet attacks; Sect. 7 argues the trade-off between services, security and user rights; and finally in Sect. 8, we draw our conclusions and cover directions for future work.

2 Privacy

Although many security attacks became more prevalent and much more dangerous due to the nature of OSNs, user privacy is the most studied problem. Maybe this is due to the fact that many attacks that lead to privacy infringement do not require any sophisticated technical knowledge. Moreover, the weaknesses of privacy techniques might cause serious implications on one's life and some private information disclosure can affect the users' future opportunities as well [42].

Many researchers presented models to protect privacy, some focused on the role of the social network sites while other focused on giving control to users over their privacy. Section 2.1 discusses user-based privacy protection while Sect. 2.2 discusses anonymization as a provider-based privacy protection.

2.1 User-Based Privacy Protection

The majority of OSN platforms provide privacy protection mechanisms which mainly depend on giving the user the capability to set his/her privacy preferences. Several similar approaches can be found in the literature; for instance, the work given in [9] shows a method which lets users dictate the privacy policy of their information combined with encrypting private attributes. Unfortunately, these methods depend heavily on the knowledge and awareness of users.

It is argued that even well-informed users overlook many possible threats to their own privacy, especially since the details of policies and practices controlling privacy are usually hidden by OSNs intentionally for the purpose of maximizing sign up rates and increasing profit [16]. An interesting case study on this matter shows that even users concerned with their online privacy, adjust the privacy setting or even use nicknames, but still add personal information to their profiles [44]. Another study shows that only a minimal percentage of users actually change their permeable privacy settings [29].

Many dimensions can be involved in how personal information is disclosed; sharing different information in different sites (possibly based on the social network nature) can cause personal information to be collected from those multiple sites [37].

Exploiting privacy can also be done by automated identity theft [13]. A well-known class of attacks exploiting privacy is inference attacks where private information can be inferred from public information; a possible scenario is shown in Fig. 1. A convincing methodology of how an attacker can predict private information from publicly available attributes is presented in [30, 55].

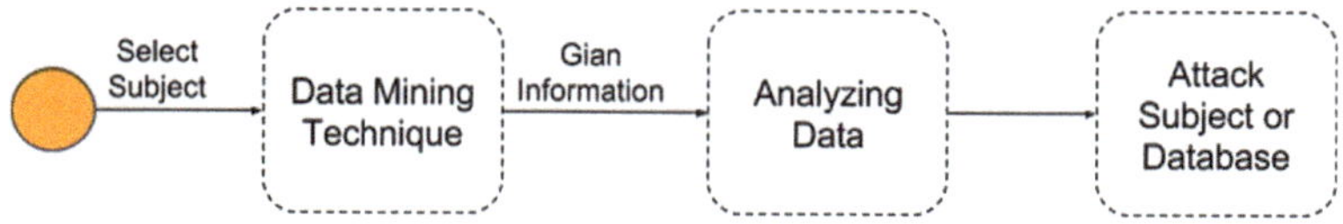

Fig. 1 Inference attacks

2.2 Anonymization and De-anonymization

One method to preserve privacy is anonymization which aims to make activities unlinkable to a single person or device [14]. The analysis of online activities is needed for many stakeholders; an apparent example is the national policy and security organizations who have to focus their attention on the actions taken within the virtual world [45].

Anonymization is a hard task to do; in order to make information mining more effective, anonymization methods keep information about the structure and the data of the OSN private as much as possible. Therefore, and as one might expect, this method has a reversing process which is to perform a re-identification of the anonymized network. A class of de-anonymization attacks has been a particular research topic [24].

Although there are procedures for hiding the structure of the network such as changing the size and the network properties, some studies show that it is still possible to infer the structure of the original network. Truta et al. [43] studied the difference between the original network and the anonymized network in terms of the graph metrics (centrality measures, radius, diameter, etc.); the findings show similarities between the original graphs and their corresponding anonymized versions.

In [1], anonymization methods for publishing data on OSNs are categorized into three categories: one that preserves identity; another one that preserves links; and finally, ones that preserves sensitive attributes. For an anonymized network to be useful there should be some attribute that is measured and that is similar to the original network.

Backstrom et al. [7] argue that in anonymization methods preserving links, only a single anonymized copy of the social network is needed for an attacker to specify whether edges exist or not between specific targeted pairs of nodes. Additionally, a de-anonymization algorithm that depends on the network topology is proposed [40, 49, 56].

Chester and Srivastava [20] propose a method to combat the attribute disclosure attacks by ensuring that the label distribution in every neighborhood of the graph is close to that throughout the entire network.

Anonymization and de-anonymization is a hot research topic since finding information from a social network is necessary and maintaining privacy in the process is not easily achievable, especially since the application of mining social networks requires those networks to hold some true beneficial data.

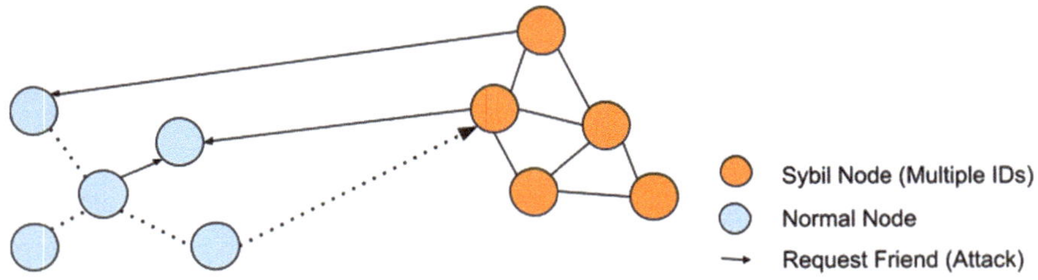

Fig. 2 Sybil attack

3 Sybil Attack

In this type of attack, the attacker uses a large number of identities in order to gain influence (see Fig. 2). Being vulnerable to Sybil attacks has to do with the way users make registration or how identities are generated. Taking into account the nature of OSNs and the openness of the system, it is assumed that large-scale Sybil attacks are practically possible.

Most solutions to protect users against Sybil attacks assume that it is feasible by default, so suggestions depend on the network structure and topology to identify the attackers. The work proposed in [46] is an example of a system that leverages the network topologies to defend against Sybil attacks in social networks. An analysis effort of characterizing such attacks is given in [52].

Danezis et al. [22] label social network nodes as honest or Sybil-controlled based on a probabilistic model and an inference engine that returns potential regions of Sybil-controlled nodes. Another approach that limits the corruptive influences of Sybil attacks where attackers can create many identities but with few trust relationships is proposed by Yu et al. [53].

A survey on the evolution of Sybil defense protocols that are based on social graph structures is presented in [5]; the survey highlights the relation between Sybil defense and the theory of random walks. The authors add a new goal for Sybil defense which is securely white-listing a local region of the graph.

4 Social Engineering Attacks

In this attack type, the attacker plans to build trust and sense of safety with the victim in order to make the victim help the attacker in one way or in another [41]. The steps of a typical social engineering attack are depicted inn Fig. 3.

A feasible attack is to convince the victim to contact the attacker, which results in increasing trust between them. In addition to traditional resources utilized by social engineers such as emails, company websites and phone calls, OSNs provide a very convenient channel for social engineers. Utilizing OSNs, attackers can easily

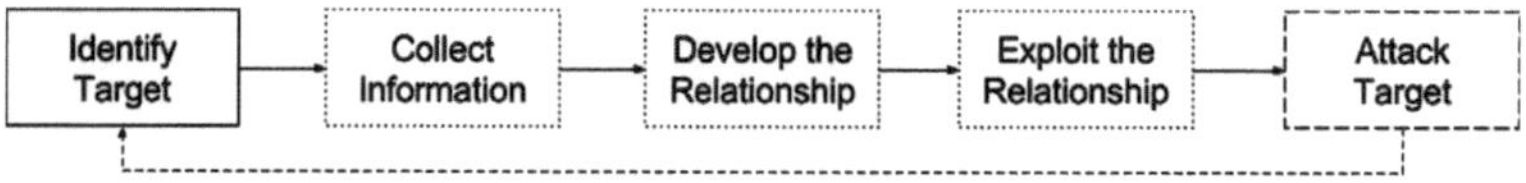

Fig. 3 Social engineering attacks

create fake profiles, harvest personal information and explore the complex sharing model of these platforms. Another major advantage provided by OSNs is the large number of targets who can be reached in a short period of time [38]. The attacker will not need any special knowledge or tools; one simple method is to use the friend- finding features available in many OSNs which is proved to be effective in practice [31].

Mouton et al. [39] described an attack with several scenarios in which attackers can use an OSN to perform social engineering attacks. For instance, an attacker may analyze the attribute of some public profiles in a particular OSN in order to create customized spam emails. Also, he/she can create fake profiles to share shortened URLs linked to malware-infected websites controlled by the attacker. Another family of social engineering attacks in the context on OSNs was discussed in [34]. These attacks are based on exploiting the mutual friends feature of many popular platforms such as Facebook and LikedIn. Accordingly, attackers can find out friends and distant neighbors of the targeted users. This represents a privacy attack against users who do not want to disclose such information.

5 Spam

Although spam is mostly recognized in emails [4], OSN users suffer heavily from spam and spammers. Spam can be of different forms; sometimes by sending unwanted messages such as advertisements, and sometimes by sending messages repeatedly to the same destination [18].

Research in detecting spam can be categorized by the features used in the detection process. Work done in [12] detects spam by analyzing the social graph between users and pages and the times at which the edges in the graph (the 'likes') were created. Another similar graph-based approach [2] represents users' profiles as nodes and their interactions as the graph edges. The weight of an edge is based on the real social interactions in terms of active friends, page likes and shared URLs.

Wu et al. argue [50] that existing studies tend to consider social spammer detection and spam message detection as two different tasks; however, both of them have an inherent connection. After all, the social spammers have a high chance to send spam messages; also, the spam messages will be posted by the social spammers. Hence, having a method that considers both detections has the possibility to improve the performance of the two tasks. They combine both detection approaches by utilizing the posting relations between messages and users, then extract these social relations to improve the detection results.

In one of our current research project we are working toward developing a model to detect spam in the context of Twitter. Our approach is based on extracting publicly available features such as the existence of suspicious words, tweets frequency and time, the existence of hyperlinks and other features. Based on the extracted features we are planning to test various machine learning classifiers together with an optimization algorithm in order to improve our detection method.

6 Malware and Botnets

As we discussed earlier, OSNs made many attacks more dangerous. Malware is a good example where the propagation and speed of attacks become more complicated. The propagation of malware in OSNs is studied in [19]. Cheng et al. propose an analytical model which can be used to measure the propagation speed and severity of malwares with various settings of infection rates and average node degrees in social networks. They claim that such a model can be utilized to develop detection strategies to avoid large-scale malware attacks. Figure 4 shows an example of a malware attack.

Attackers can use malware to create a very large controlled network consisting of victims' machines. Such a network is referred to as a Command and Control (CC) or Robotic Network (Botnet). Botnets depend on a network of computers. The attacker basically controls computers in the network to achieve goals such as sending spam or participating in distributed Denial-of-Service (DoS) attacks. Computers participating in an attack can communicate by message passing or by building a command and control architecture. Farina et al. [23] analyzed the possibility of executing distributed DoS attacks from mobile phones. They introduced the SlowBot Net concept where mobile agents are involved in the infrastructure design. In their work, a SlowBot Net was compared to the well-known internet botnet called Low-Orbit Ion Cannon (LOIC) that is adopted by hackers who break into computer systems for political or social purposes (called cyber-hacktivists) and proved that the attacker in a SlowBot Net needs a lesser number of resources and that it can be easily deployed on mobile nodes. Kartaltepe et al. [35] envision the possibilities of using OSNs in botnet attacks that are built over the command and control architecture of botnet attacks. Athanasopoulos et al. [6] show how to use Facebook as an attack platform.

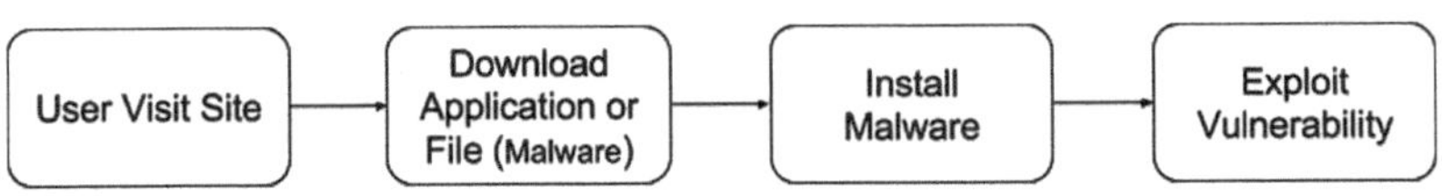

Fig. 4 Malware attacks

In order to find suspicious bot actions in Twitter, graph-based analysis was applied [51]. To narrow the nodes possibly passing bots, Peri-Watchdog was applied to OSNs. After running Peri-Watchdog on some datasets core stability was observed in the OSN. Boshmaf et al. [17], evaluated how a Socialbot Network (SbN) can infiltrate OSNs. They found that using bots to imitate Facebook can largely infiltrate this OSN (Facebook), especially if there are mutual friends between bots and users. Additionally, it is difficult for socialbots to offer any defense (stop or detect an SbN) to OSNs which has a negative impact on privacy breaches and has serious implications for software systems that are socially aware.

7 Services, Security, and Stakeholders' Rights

In this part of the chapter, we will discuss the different viewpoints of how the security and privacy of social networks is perceived and how it is managed so far. We chose the title of this section to be services, security, and stakeholders' rights since there is a conflict between many of the services provided by OSNs and security (we assume here that privacy is part of the security concept). We also add rights to the title since the disagreement over what should be done and what is allowed to be done lies in how one perceives the stakeholders' rights. All the possible trade-offs and possibly solutions to different issues can be applied if the rights and responsibilities of stakeholders are determined.

The responsibility of users' privacy is somewhat unknown; some people think the end user must be responsible for their own privacy, while others think social media sites are the ones responsible. It is hard to determine the rights and responsibilities of different stakeholders in OSNs.

Many researchers consider monitoring users' online behavior a positive thing since this monitoring can result in better, more focused services and can enhance the user experience [33]. Furthermore, monitoring can be used to detect security threats and anomalies [36] which would help in protecting privacy.

Many research works discuss techniques to analyze behavior [11] or even predict future behavior such as finding possible links the user might be interested in, or more likely to connect to in the future [8, 25, 54].

Privacy policies usually generalize and give rights to the OSN owner. The user might not consider the terms of a privacy policy as a threat to his/her own privacy at the time of sign up and registration. Additionally, policies are usually hidden by the OSN site to increase profit and the number of users.

Therefore, we are talking about rights. The security measures taken into consideration by an OSN might violate what may be considered as an end user right. One of the solutions to the privacy issues is to find a balance that satisfies the needs of all stakeholders. An important question is how such balance can be achieved in reality.

All in all, there are many technical steps that can be taken in practice, but there should be some form of regulation that distinguishes the rights of OSN owners, third party service providers, end users and governments.

8 Conclusion and Future Work

In this chapter, we discussed some of the current research in the field of online social networks security. We presented different attacks that are especially relevant to online social networks. Moreover, we highlighted some methods and precautions available to tackle these attacks. A discussion of the tradeoff between services and security was also given in the light of stakeholders' rights and responsibilities.

Accordingly, we argue that there is a need for suggesting models and technical solutions in the light of the emerging threats that we highlighted in this chapter. Recommendations to mitigate each kind of threat can be furnished together with the proper action that should be taken in case these threats occur. Possible future directions—categorized based on the attacks discussed—include:

- Privacy: most of the attractive features over various types of OSN depend on processing user personal information such as location, age, gender, emotion, click stream and other online behavioral characteristics. Privacy typically means giving the user control over all his personal information, which is usually provided to the users thorough a configurable privacy policy. However, other aspects include the right to be alone which is sometimes called spatial privacy and the protection of personal information during processing by or exchanged between OSNs. Such issues might need further investigation.
- Sybil attack: Alqatawna [3] proposes behavioral biometrics as a method for continuous authentication over OSNs. The same idea can be adapted for detecting fake accounts belonging to the same malicious user. Users over OSNs perform various activities including posting, sharing, downloading, and uploading. This makes such platforms extremely interactive and such user activities create a huge amount of information with strong personal and behavioral characteristics which can be utilized to identify criminals with Sybil accounts.
- Social engineering: one research direction to be suggested here is the development of effective built-in security awareness methods for OSNs. These methods should be usable as much as possible and naturally integrated with the graphical user interface of a particular OSN.

References

1. Adusumalli SK, Vatsavayi VK, Vadisala J (2014) A study of privacy attacks on social network data. J Glob Res Comput Sci 5(7):12–18
2. Ahmed F, Abulaish M (2012) An mcl-based approach for spam profile detection in online social networks. In: 11th International conference on trust, security and privacy in computing and communications (TrustCom), 2012. IEEE, pp 602–608
3. Alqatawna J (2015) An adaptive multimodal biometric framework for intrusion detection in online social networks. IJCSNS Int J Comput Sci Netw Secur 15(4):19–25
4. Alqatawna J, Faris H, Jaradat K, Al-Zewairi M, Adwan O (2015) Improving knowledge based spam detection methods: the effect of malicious related features in imbalance data distribution. Int J Commun Netw Syst Sci 8:118–129
5. Alvisi L, Clement A, Epasto A, Lattanzi S, Panconesi A (2013) Sok: the evolution of sybil defense via social networks. In: 2013 IEEE Symposium on security and privacy (SP), pp 382–396
6. Athanasopoulos E, Makridakis A, Antonatos S, Antoniades D, Ioannidis S, Anagnostakis KG, Markatos EP (2008) Antisocial networks: turning a social network into a botnet. In: Information security. Springer, New york, pp 146–160
7. Backstrom L, Dwork C, Kleinberg J (2007) Wherefore art thou r3579x?: anonymized social net- works, hidden patterns, and structural steganography. In: Proceedings of the 16th international conference on World Wide Web. ACM, pp 181–190
8. Backstrom L, Leskovec J (2011) Supervised random walks: predicting and recommending links in social networks. In: Proceedings of the fourth ACM international conference on web search and data mining, WSDM'11. ACM, New York, NY, USA, pp 635–644
9. Baden R, Bender A, Spring N, Bhattacharjee B, Starin D (2009) Persona: an online social network with user-defined privacy. SIGCOMM Comput Commun Rev 39(4):135–146
10. Beach A, Gartrell M, Han R (2009) Solutions to security and privacy issues in mobile social networking. In: Computational science and engineering, 2009, CSE'09, vol. 4, pp 1036–1042
11. Benevenuto F, Rodrigues T, Cha M, Almeida V (2012) Characterizing user navigation and in- teractions in online social networks. Inf Sci 195:1–24
12. Beutel A, Xu W, Guruswami V, Palow C, Faloutsos C (2013) Copycatch: stopping group attacks by spotting lockstep behavior in social networks. In: Proceedings of the 22nd international conference on World Wide Web international World Wide Web conferences steering committee, pp 119–130
13. Bilge L, Strufe T, Balzarotti D, Kirda E (2009) All your contacts are belong to us: automated identity theft attacks on social networks. In: Proceedings of the 18th international conference on World Wide Web, WWW'09. ACM, New York, NY, USA, pp 551–560
14. Biskup J (2009) Security in computing systems: challenges, approaches and solutions, anonymization. Springer, Heidelberg, pp 513–525
15. Bodriagov O, Buchegger S (2011) Encryption for peer-to-peer social networks. In: Third inernational conference on privacy, security, risk and trust (PASSAT) and social computing (socialcom), 2011. IEEE, pp 1302–1309
16. Bonneau J, Preibusch S (2010) Economics of information security and privacy. the privacy jungle:on the market for data protection in social networks. Springer, Boston, pp 121–167
17. Boshmaf Y, Muslukhov I, Beznosov K, Ripeanu M (2013) Design and analysis of a social botnet. Comput Netw 57(2):556–578
18. Chakraborty M, Pal S, Pramanik R, Chowdary CR (2016) Recent developments in social spam detection and combating techniques: a survey. Inf Process Manag
19. Cheng SM, Ao WC, Chen PY, Chen KC (2011) On modeling malware propagation in generalized social networks. IEEE Commun Lett 15(1):25–27
20. Chester S, Srivastava G (2011) Social network privacy for attribute disclosure attacks. In: 2011 International conference on advances in social networks analysis and mining (ASONAM). IEEE, pp 445–449

21. Cutillo LA, Molva R, Strufe T (2009) Safebook: a privacy-preserving online social network leveraging on real-life trust. IEEE Commun Mag 47(12):94–101
22. Danezis G, Mittal P (2009) Sybilinfer: detecting sybil nodes using social networks. In: NDSS. San Diego, CA
23. Farina P, Cambiaso E, Papaleo G, Aiello M (2016) Are mobile botnets a possible threat? the case of slowbot net. Comput Secur 58:268–283
24. Fernandes DAB, Soares LFB, Gomes JV, Freire MM, Inácio PRM (2014) Security issues in cloud environments: a survey. Int J Inf Secur 13(2):113–170
25. Fire M, Tenenboim L, Lesser O, Puzis R, Rokach L, Elovici Y (2011) Link prediction in social networks using computationally efficient topological features. In: Third inernational conference on privacy, security, risk and trust (PASSAT) and social computing (SocialCom), 2011 IEEE, pp 73–80
26. Gao H, Hu J, Huang T, Wang J, Chen Y (2011) Security issues in online social networks. IEEE Int Comput 15(4):56–63
27. Goolsby R, Shanley L, Lovell A (2013) On cybersecurity, crowdsourcing, and social cyber-attack. Technical. Report, DTIC document
28. Graffi K, Mukherjee P, Menges B, Hartung D, Kovacevic A, Steinmetz R (2009) Practical security in p 2p-based social networks. In: 34th Conference on local computer networks, 2009, LCN 2009. IEEE, pp 269–272
29. Gross R, Acquisti A (2005) Information revelation and privacy in online social networks. In: Proceedings of the 2005 ACM workshop on privacy in the electronic society, WPES'05. ACM, New York, NY, USA, pp 71–80
30. Heatherly R, Kantarcioglu M, Thuraisingham B (2013) Preventing private information inference attacks on social networks. IEEE Trans Knowl Data Eng 25(8):1849–1862
31. Irani D, Balduzzi M, Balzarotti D, Kirda E, Pu C (2011) Reverse social engineering attacks in online social networks. In: Detection of intrusions and malware, and vulnerability assessment. Springer, New York, pp 55–74
32. Jahid S, Nilizadeh S, Mittal P, Borisov N, Kapadia A (2012) Decent: a decentralized architecture for enforcing privacy in online social networks. In: International conference on pervasive computing and communications workshops (PERCOM workshops), 2012. IEEE, pp 326–332
33. Jin L, Chen Y, Wang T, Hui P, Vasilakos AV (2013) Understanding user behavior in online social networks: a survey. IEEE Commun Mag 51(9):144–150
34. Jin L, Joshi JB, Anwar M (2013) Mutual-friend based attacks in social network systems. Comput secur 37:15–30
35. Kartaltepe EJ, Morales JA, Xu S, Sandhu R (2010) Applied cryptography and network security In: 8th International conference, ACNS 2010, Beijing, China, June 22–25, 2010. Proceedings, social network-based botnet command-and-control: emerging threats and countermeasures. Springer, Heidelberg, pp 511–528
36. Kaur R, Singh S (2015) A survey of data mining and social network analysis based anomaly detection techniques. Egypt Inf J
37. Krishnamurthy B, Wills CE (2009) On the leakage of personally identifiable information via online social networks. In: Proceedings of the 2nd ACM workshop on online social networks, WOSN'09. ACM, New York, NY, USA, pp 7–12
38. Krombholz K, Hobel H, Huber M, Weippl E (2015) Advanced social engineering attacks. J Inf Secur Appl 22:113–122
39. Mouton F, Leenen L, Venter H (2016) Social engineering attack examples, templates and scenarios. Comput Secur 59:186–209
40. Narayanan A, Shmatikov V (2009) De-anonymizing social networks. In: 30th IEEE Symposium on security and privacy, 2009. IEEE, pp 173–187
41. Puneeth M, Farha JS, Yamini M, Sandhya N (2015) Social engineering on social networking sites. Int J Adv Eng Res Sci (IJAERS) 2(6):58–60
42. Rosenblum D (2007) What anyone can know: the privacy risks of social networking sites. IEEE Secur Priv 5(3):40–49

43. Truta TM, Campan A, Gasmi A, Cooper N, Elstun A (2011) Centrality preservation in anonymized social networks. In: Proceedings of the international conference on data mining (DMIN11)
44. Tufekci Z (2008) Can you see me now? audience and disclosure regulation in online social network sites. Bull Sci Technol Soc 28(1):20–36
45. Weber RH, Heinrich UI (2012) Anonymization, limitations of anonymization. Springer, London, pp 45–71
46. Wei W, Xu F, Tan CC, Li Q (2013) Sybildefender: a defense mechanism for sybil attacks in large social networks. IEEE Trans Parall Distrib Syst 24(12):2492–2502
47. Weir GR, Toolan F, Smeed D (2011) The threats of social networking: old wine in new bottles? Information Security Technical Report. Soc Netw Threats 16(2):38–43
48. Williams J (2010) Social networking applications in health care: threats to the privacy and security of health information. In: Proceedings of the 2010 ICSE workshop on software engineering in health care, SEHC'10. ACM, New York, NY, USA, pp 39–49
49. Wondracek G, Holz T, Kirda E, Kruegel C (2010) A practical attack to de-anonymize social network users. In: IEEE Symposium on security and privacy (SP), 2010, IEEE, pp 223–238
50. Wu F, Shu J, Huang Y, Yuan Z (2016) Co-detecting social spammers and spam messages in microblogging via exploiting social contexts. Neurocomputing (2016)
51. Yan, G.: Peri-watchdog: hunting for hidden botnets in the periphery of online social networks. Comput Netw 57(2):540–555 (2013)
52. Yang Z, Wilson C, Wang X, Gao T, Zhao BY, Dai Y (2011) Uncovering social network sybils in the wild. In: Proceedings of the 2011 ACM SIGCOMM conference on internet measurement conference, IMC'11. ACM, New York, NY, USA, pp 259–268
53. Yu H, Kaminsky M, Gibbons PB, Flaxman A (2006) Sybilguard: defending against sybil attacks via social networks. ACM SIGCOMM Comput Commun Rev 36(4):267–278
54. Zhao Z, Feng S, Wang Q, Huang JZ, Williams GJ, Fan J (2012) Topic oriented community detection through social objects and link analysis in social networks. Knowl Based Syst 26:164–173
55. Zheleva E, Getoor L (2009) To join or not to join: the illusion of privacy in social networks with mixed public and private user profiles. In: Proceedings of the 18th International Conference on World Wide Web, WWW'09. ACM, New York, NY, USA, pp 531–540
56. Zhu T, Wang S, Li X, Zhou Z, Zhang R (2013) Structural attack to anonymous graph of social networks. Math Probl Eng 2013

Kolibri 360 GmbH
Ferdinand-Jühlke-Straße 7
99095 Erfurt, Deutschland
produktsicherheit@kolibri360.de